Cult

W9-AJT-472

SEX & SENSIBILITY

*Reflections on
Forbidden Mirrors and
the Will to Censor*

Marcia Pally

THE ECCO PRESS

Copyright © 1994 by Marcia Pally
All rights reserved

THE ECCO PRESS
100 West Broad Street
Hopewell, New Jersey 08525
Published simultaneously in Canada by
Penguin Books Canada Ltd., Ontario
Printed in the United States of America

Designed by Richard Oriolo

FIRST EDITION

Library of Congress Cataloging-in-Publication Data

Pally, Marcia.
Sex & sensibility : reflection on forbidden mirrors and the will to
censor / by Marcia Pally.
p.   cm.
1. Censorship—United States.   2. Sex in mass media—
Censorship—United States.   3. Violence in mass media—
Censorship—United States.   4. Freedom of speech—United States.
I. Title.   II. Title: Sex and sensibility.
Z658.U5P36   1994
363.3'1'0973—dc20   93-40142
ISBN 0-88001-364-8

The text of this book is set in Perpetua

ACKNOWLEDGMENTS

Before anyone else and in critical ways, my agent Philip Pochoda and my friend and teacher Dennis Sayers nudged me when I needed it, and gave me a way to write this book. My thanks to my publishers, Jeanne Carter and Dan Halpern, who believed in the project, and to all the people at The Ecco Press for shepherding it through the process of publishing.

I am indebted to the women of Feminists for Free Expression (FFE). Their belief in the First Amendment, their understanding that it is essential for feminism, carried me through the founding of that organization and the writing of this book. I am grateful especially to Nadine Strossen, Cathy Crosson, Candida Royalle, Marilyn Fitterman, Wendy Kaminer, Karen De Crow, Amelia Arenas, Sandy

Rapp, Cynthia Gentry, Marjorie Heins, and the Board of Directors of FFE—Lavada Blanton, Patti Britton, Jennifer Maguire, Beth Nathanson, Catherine Siemann, Joan Kennedy Taylor, and Trish Moylan Torruella.

I have relied on the research of many friends and colleagues over the years, and on their commitment to freedom of expression. I would like to thank Peter Bloch, Judy Blume, Bob Chatelle, F.M. Christensen, Betty Dodson, Edward De Grazia, Edward Donnerstein, Betty Friedan, Bob Guccione, Nat Hentoff, John Irving, Penn Jilette, Erica Jong, Burt Joseph, Kathy Keeton, Marty Klein, Stuart Klawans, Judith Krug, Gail Markels, David Myerson, Jim Peterson, James M. Saslow, Joseph Scott, Vans Stevenson, Larry Sutter, Teller, Teri Tomcisin, and Tom Wicker. For their skills in computer research and copy editing, and for their forbearance, I would like to thank Daniel Jussim, Lisa Goodkin, Elizabeth Ellis and Ann Horowitz.

I am deeply grateful to the boards of Americans for Constitutional Freedom and The Freedom to Read Foundation who published an earlier version of portions of this book. Thanks also to the many people who worked on that project, especially Cleo Wilson, Cindy Rakowitz, Jill Chuckerman, John Dixon, Carmen Armillas, and Arlan Bushman. Special thanks goes to Sue Dickey for her good spirits in the face of arcane requests and to Bari Nash for her tireless fact checking.

Finally, I wish to thank Pam for sticking by me through all the trials, error, and paper; my parents and teachers at the Solomon Schechter School, who taught me that without tolerance we have only thuggery; and the bracing vision of the Constitution which inspires and cheers me.

CONTENTS

PREFACE

> The First Amendment was designed "to invite
> dispute," to induce "a condition of unrest," to
> "create dissatisfaction with conditions as they
> are," and even to stir "people to anger."
>   The First Amendment was not fashioned as a
> vehicle for dispensing tranquilizers to the people.
> Its prime function was to keep debate open to
> "offensive" as well as to "staid" people . . . the
> materials before us may be garbage. But so is
> much of what is said in political campaigns, in the
> daily press, on tv, or over the radio. By reason of
> the First Amendment . . . speakers and publishers
> have not been threatened or subdued because
> their thoughts and ideas may be "offensive" to
> some.
>
> —Justice William O. Douglas, *Miller v. California*

Supreme Court Justice William Douglas takes it as an obvious good that "speakers and publishers have not been threatened or subdued." The rights to free expression have been considered a foundation of democracy, censorship an incursion into liberty. These rights were meant most particularly to protect unpopular material, those words and images some people believe are dangerous, blasphemous, or offensive. In addition to its historical role in framing our system of government, the First Amendment more recently was the linchpin of the civil rights movement's challenge to racial discrimination, which many Americans at first considered lunatic and anarchic. It is why Christian fundamentalists may promote their wish for a Bible-based government. It allows white supremacists to publicize their views, deficit-spending economists to promote theirs, and women to challenge sexism and gender roles—though most Americans are not Christian fundamentalists, deficit spenders, white supremacists, or feminists.

From time to time legislators, community groups, and other participants in public life believe there is benefit in subduing speakers and publishers and the material they bring before the nation. Society will profit, they reason, from shaping for the good the ideas its people encounter. During the first Reagan administration, such shaping found new support. Enthusiasts promised no loss in works of value and pledged to oust the really gruesome, horrible stuff. This would reduce drug abuse, teen pregnancy, violence and sexual violence, it was argued. Chapter one briefly lists some works that have earned the attention of this campaign.

Chapter two of this volume introduces the main proponents of censorship in the United States, some of the reasons censorship is attractive as social policy, and historical evidence that belies the accuracy of blaming words and images for social ills. Chapters three and seven review the social science data on sexual material, violent material and the commission of crimes, and methodological problems that limit the findings.

Chapter four discusses three popular arguments for censorship: that taxpayers should not be compelled to spend their dollars on words and images they dislike and so certain artworks should not be publicly funded; that the "porn made me do it" excuse is a reasonable alibi for criminal conduct; and that communities have the right to expel from their midsts words and images they believe are offensive or dangerous. Chapter five looks at popular feminist arguments for the censorship of sexually explicit material. Chapter six investigates two claims: first, that performers in the sex industries are abused and exploited more than workers elsewhere, and second, that the solution to this abuse is to ban sexual material and close down those industries.

Chapter eight discusses the role of fiction and fantasy in human society and the individual imagination. It reviews the effectiveness of labeling systems in reducing violent conduct, and suggests policy measures to address sexual and nonsexual violence that do not rely on book, movie, and music banning. Chapter nine considers more fully the appeal of censorship efforts to individuals and community groups. It looks also at censorship's appeal to some feminists, and examines the recent "victim culture" that has developed in certain feminist circles. Chapter ten looks at the hate speech movement on university campuses and suggests ways to combat offensive, discriminatory speech without silencing the speaker.

One

MR. BOWDLER'S RETURN ENGAGEMENT
Recent Censorship Efforts

By the end of the 1980s, book banning had increased to three times the levels of 1979, according to the Office for Intellectual Freedom of the American Library Association (ALA). The most censored books included *Anne Frank: The Diary of a Young Girl*, *To Kill a Mockingbird*, *Of Mice and Men*, *1984*, *Slaughterhouse-Five*, *Catcher in the Rye*, *The Adventures of Huckleberry Finn*, all the works of Stephen King and Judy Blume (especially Blume's *Are You There, God? It's Me, Margaret*—for mentioning menstruation), the children's book *The Sisters Impossible* (for the words *hell* and *fart*), Studs Terkel's *Working*, Desmond Morris's *The Naked Ape*, Alice Walker's *The Color Purple*, and the following dictionaries: *Webster's Seventh*, *Random House*, *Doubleday*, and *American Heritage* (for including definitions of "dirty" words). Among the films and videotapes removed from library and store shelves between 1980 and 1990 were *A Passage to India, Victor/Victoria, A Clockwork Orange,* Zeffirelli's *Romeo and Juliet,* and *Splash!*

In 1992, the ALA reported a 28 percent increase in book-banning efforts above the increases seen through the 1980s, though the ALA estimates that 85 percent of censorship efforts go unreported (Granberry, 1993). Judith Krug, director of the ALA's Office for Intellectual Freedom, expected 1993 levels to be higher. People for the American Way reported in 1992 a 50 percent increase in censorship in the public schools, the greatest rise in book-banning efforts in a decade. In 41 percent of cases, efforts to ban or restrict books were successful (Jordan, 1992). Joining the list of most frequently targeted books are John Steinbeck's *The Grapes of Wrath* and Madeleine L'Engle's *A Wrinkle in Time.*

According to the ALA, the fastest-growing area of book censorship in 1991 was the occult; the second fastest was health and family life issues, particularly works addressing AIDS education, sex education, and drug abuse. By 1993, the emphasis had shifted, with attacks against materials believed to be occult taking second place to challenges against AIDS education, sex education, and discussions of homosexuality. People for the American Way found that the most frequent reason for censorship efforts is the belief that material contains objectionable sexual references, is at odds with the challenger's religious views, or is "new age" or anti-Christian (Jordan, 1992).

In Riverside County, California, a school principal removed Maya Angelou's *I Know Why the Caged Bird Sings* from one class's reading list for its sexual references. The offending passage recounts the sexual assault Angelou suffered as a girl, which left her mute for nearly a decade (Granberry, 1993). For the same reason, the book was attacked in Raleigh, North Carolina; Bremerton, Washington; Lafayette, Louisiana; and Strong, Maine. A Monroe County, Michigan, library director enjoyed months of attacks by local decency groups for carrying Madonna's *Sex* on public library shelves. At community meetings and in statements to the press, he said libraries service all sectors of the Monroe County population, including the many adults who wished to borrow Madonna's book. For his words, he received threats of physical violence both at his office and home. Threats then turned to his five-year-old son (Conable, 1991; 1993). In Carson City, Nevada, the State Board of Education met to determine whether *Rolling Stone* magazine should be banned from school libraries statewide. In Meridian, Ohio, Citizens for Excellence in Education threatened to sue a school district for teaching students about AIDS prevention. Education officials there issued a gag order to stop all AIDS prevention classes. A California school district was taken to court by the American Family Association (AFA) to prevent the district from using the celebrated Impressions reading series. The AFA held that the chapter on Halloween, with its witches and goblins, constituted the "religion" of satanism (American Family Association Journal, 1991).

The AFA boycotted Pepsi for advertising on MTV; it boycotted Burger King for taking ads on *Tour of Duty,* a CBS made-for-TV movie which the AFA felt contained "profane language and graphic violence." The subject of *Tour of Duty* is the war in Vietnam. The AFA boycotted the Pfizer Corporation for advertising on *Cheers,* a show that AFA Director Rev. Donald Wildmon wrote, "pushes sexual perversions." These "perversions" refer to an episode in which a couple tries to have a baby and the wife discusses, according to the AFA, "her ovaries and Fallopian tubes." The AFA attacked *The Allison Gertz Story,* a TV movie about the teenager who spent the last years of her life as an AIDS educator before dying from the disease. The film won the Secretary's Award for Excellence in Public Service and Health from Louis Sullivan, then Health and Human Services Secretary. The AFA charged *I'll Fly Away* with "abundant profanity," teen sex, and adultery. The program won the prestigious Humanitas Prize for its sensitive presentation of racial issues (Dreifus, 1992).

According to Know Censorship, which produces a quarterly publication tracking and analyzing criminal obscenity prosecutions, over 2,000 book and movie titles have been prosecuted since 1987. Federal courts have seen 50 trials since that year; Know Censorship has identified over 300 cases in state courts, only a portion of the total that can be found by filing Freedom of Information Act requests in the 3,000 counties of the United States. Jeffrey Douglas, the criminal defense attorney who compiles Know Censorship's data base, notes in his research (Douglas, 1993) the lack of pattern in the titles prosecuted "even within one county. It calls into question the notion of 'community standard' as a test of obscenity." He notes also the high rate (over 90 percent) of convictions "but not through trials, through pleas of guilty."

"The usual sequence of events," Douglas said, "goes like this: A cop goes into a book or video store, finds something that offends him, and charges the owner with obscenity. Most retailers can't afford to go to trial so they plead guilty and pay a fine. That title is then declared obscene and prohibited from distribution in that area, without any judicial or community review. It becomes a matter of the decision of one cop. Additionally, that retailer has pled guilty to a crime that triggers the racketeering laws, which on a second charge permit the government to seize and destroy the defendant's full stock and equipment. Even if a state doesn't have a racketeering law at the time of conviction, should it pass one, it is retroactive ten years."

Efforts to restrict material have come not only from conservatives. The National Coalition on Television Violence (NCTV), a group with liberal credentials, has been active in ferreting out material it believes endangers the public. Not only does the NCTV censure movies like *The Texas Chainsaw Massacre 2,* it also cites in its bulletins films such as *Star Trek IV: The Voyage Home* for "chasing, gun threat, and one Vulcan nerve pinch." NCTV cites the animated cartoon *Lady and the Tramp* and the popular Christmas ballet *The Nutcracker* for its "battle between soldiers and mice." Included in NCTV's list of objectionable books are the works of Stephen King, Robert Ludlum, Frederick Forsyth, Mario Puzo, James Clavell, Helen MacInnes, John le Carré, and Leon Uris (National Coalition on Television Violence Newsletters, 1987–92; see for example March 14, 1988; see also Peterson, 1987).

Reflecting on the value of the First Amendment, Supreme Court Justice Louis Brandeis wrote, "The greatest dangers to liberty lurk in the insidious enchroachment by men of zeal, well-meaning but without understanding" (*Olmstead v. United States,* 1928). The men and women of good will who promised to remove only the most noxious material appear to have extended their platform.

CENSORSHIP EFFORTS

A sampling of censorship efforts in schools, libraries, the media, and the arts between 1988 and 1993 (for a historical overview of censorship see Walter Kendrick's *The Secret Museum*, 1987; special emphasis on the censorship of blasphemy can be found in *Blasphemy: Verbal Offense Against the Sacred*, by Leonard Levy; for an overview of censorship and the arts in this century, see Edward De Grazia's *Girls Lean Back Everywhere: The Law of Obscenity and the Assault on Genius*, 1992, and Marjorie Heins's *Sex, Sin, and Blasphemy: A Guide to America's Censorship Wars*, 1993a).

1993

• The Justice Department went to court to uphold the "decency" requirements on grants awarded by the National Endowment for the Arts (NEA). Appealing a federal court ruling that had declared the "decency" standard unconstitutional, the government claimed that requiring NEA judges to consider "decency" as part of the artistic merit of each application was within constitutional bounds. To make its case, the Justice Department relied on the precedent set in *Rust v. Sullivan* (known as the "gag rule" abortion counseling case). In *Rust*, the Supreme Court had ruled that the government may decide what information it wishes to pay for in federally funded family planning clinics. The Bush administration decided it would not permit discussions of abortion in clinics that receive government monies (the decision prohibited abortion counseling; provision of abortion services had already been proscribed).

(continued)

Making a parallel case, the Justice Department claimed that government may buy the expression it likes at the NEA as well. It argued that if it wants to fund only art that has passed a "decency" standard, it may. Sixty arts, cultural, and literary organizations filed briefs protesting the Justice Department's case (National Campaign, 1993; Trescott, 1993; Hartigan, 1993).

- The Federal Communications Commission (FCC) broadened its definition of what may not be carried on the nation's television and radio airwaves. Broadcasters have long been prohibited from airing what is "indecent," that is, programming that "depicts or describes . . . sexual or excretory activities or organs" in a "patently offensive" way according to "contemporary community standards for the medium." Broadening their prohibitions, the FCC now defines "indecent" as nonprofane sexual innuendo and double entendre. Violations of FCC "indecency" standards cost programmers strict fines, the amounts determined by the FCC with no peer or trial review (American Civil Liberties Union, Arts Censorship Project, Summer 1993).

- The University of Pittsburgh denied art student David Brown permission to show one of his paintings in an otherwise open-admission student art show. The work, *There's No Place Like Hollidaysburg,* is a surrealistic landscape that the vice chancellor of student affairs called "offensive" and "not in good taste" (American Civil Liberties Union, Arts Censorship Project, Spring 1993).

- Colgate University officials removed from a university art gallery a collection of photographs by well-known photographer Lee Friedlander. A number of women had complained that the works created a "hostile work environment." The collection included photographs of the nude figure (American Civil Liberties Union, Arts Censorship Project, Summer 1993).

- City officials in Shreveport, Louisiana, canceled a concert by the rock group Society of the Damned because they felt the concert "could be political" and that fliers for the program had created "political overtones." The concert was to be held at a public park, a location that has been recognized by the courts as a "public forum" for free debate where government may not restrict expression on political grounds. Political speech enjoys the highest constitutional protection from censorship (American Civil Liberties Union, Arts Censorship Project, Spring 1993).

- The Illinois state legislature considered a bill that would make it a crime to expose minors to any work that "counsels suicide." Booksellers, filmmakers, and librarians pointed up to legislators that the language of the bill would make it a crime to assign Shakespeare's *Romeo and Juliet* in Illinois classrooms ('Suicide' Bill, 1993).

1992

- A female instructor at a Pennsylvania college demanded that a reproduction of Goya's *Maja Desnuda* be removed from a classroom wall because it constituted sexual harassment. She was supported by the college's Commission for Women and the painting was taken down. After protests by the art department, the famous work was reinstated (Heins, 1993b; Graham-Yooll, 1992).

- The University of Michigan Law School closed an art and video exhibit commissioned by the *Michigan Journal of Gender and Law* to accompany a university conference on prostitution. The exhibit was dismantled when two conference

(continued)

CENSORSHIP EFFORTS *(cont.)*

speakers complained that some of its sexual content "would be a threat to their safety." Without informing curator Carol Jacobsen, students removed the offending videotape from the gallery; when Jacobsen explained that they could not pick apart the exhibit, they took down the rest of it (Lewin, 1992a).

- Officials in Raleigh, North Carolina, removed from a federal building a painting by Dayton Claudio because it addressed the subject of abortion. The painting was withdrawn in spite of government regulations that designate federal buildings open forums for artistic displays (American Civil Liberties Union, Arts Censorship Project, Spring 1993).

- The managers of an Express store in the Battlefield Mall in Springfield, Missouri, removed a reproduction of the Venus de Milo because, said mall manager Cheryl Beaman, "It was too shocking . . . this is a family-oriented conservative area" (*The Progressive*, 1992).

- Between 1988 and 1992, the National Endowment for the Arts (NEA) suffered repeated attacks, including the requirement that artists receiving NEA grants pledge in writing that their art would not address a list of forbidden subjects. Prohibited subject matter included not only such obvious offenses as the sexual exploitation of children but also depictions of sex and homoeroticism. Homoeroticism does not refer to homosexual sex acts but anything that might suggest a homoerotic appreciation or sensibility. Because of the many attacks on the NEA, the New York City Opera (an NEA recipient) considered dropping from its production of Arnold Schoenberg's opera *Moses und Aron* a number of scenes in which three naked virgins appear (Honan, 1991; Kozinn, 1990).

1991

- The American Family Association (AFA) launched a campaign against the TV movie *Absolute Strangers,* pressuring advertisers to pull their commercials. *Absolute Strangers* follows the efforts of a Long Island accountant, Martin Klein, to obtain an abortion, on doctors' advice, for his pregnant wife, who had gone into a coma after an auto accident. The procedure became necessary to save his wife's life. Klein was taken to court by antiabortion groups—the "absolute strangers" of the title—who sought to stop him. Klein finally obtained court permission, and his wife regained consciousness hours after the abortion was performed (Gay, 1991).
- The AFA lobbied in Congress against the NEA funding of Todd Haynes's film *Poison*, which had won first prize at the Sundance Film Festival the preceding January. This experimental film assails prejudice and the persecution of those who are different from the mainstream. It employs three allegorical stories about oppression, one based on the writings of Jean Genet about a homosexual man in prison, which the AFA called pornography (Associated Press, 1991a).
- Several states introduced bills in their legislatures that make it a crime to sell sexually related lyrics to minors. This was the first time government bodies tried to define prerecorded lyrics alone as legally obscene, making it the responsibility of local store owners and sales clerks to know the content of all the songs on all the records, tapes, and compact discs they sell, and to know in advance of selling them whether they might be prohibited to minors according to state law (Verna, 1991).
- The American Family Association campaigned against the

(continued)

CENSORSHIP EFFORTS *(cont.)*

advertisers of the television special "Our Sons." The program starred Julie Andrews and Ann-Margret as two mothers, one of whose sons is dying of AIDS (Gay, 1991).

- Blockbuster Video, the largest video retail chain in the country, dropped NC-17 films from its shelves after a boycott and pressure campaign by the American Family Association. Although Blockbuster said that none of the protests came from its video club members, the chain nevertheless scotched NC-17 material. Blockbuster told the press it dropped NC-17 videos independent of the AFA campaign, though only days before the delisting it announced that it would evaluate NC-17 tapes on a title-by-title basis (Berman, 1991; Paige, McCullaugh, & Sweeting, 1991).

1990

- The Cincinnati Contemporary Arts Center and its director, Dennis Barrie, were indicted on obscenity charges for exhibiting "The Perfect Moment," a retrospective of Robert Mapplethorpe's photography, although in that city no public monies were used to fund the show and no children under 18 were permitted entrance. Each visitor to the Cincinnati museum chose to attend the exhibit and paid for admission; each chose again to view the photographs of nudity and sexual material cordoned off in a special section that attracted the longest lines (Pally, 1990; Wilkerson, 1990).
- The rock group 2 Live Crew was indicted for obscenity, which carried not only a fine but a jail term, for an adults-only concert; admission was permitted only to those over

21 (Yardley, 1990). After a highly publicized trial, the rock group was not convicted.

- The Federal Communications Commission sought to expand its ban on adult programming from the hours when children might see such programs, 6 A.M. to 8 P.M., to the twenty-four-hour day. At no time, under such a ruling, could an adult see a radio or television program that was more sophisticated or controversial than what is appropriate for children (Andrews, 1990).

- The American Family Association persuaded General Mills, Ralston-Purina, and Domino's Pizza to withdraw advertising from *Saturday Night Live* for what AFA director Donald Wildmon called "its obsession with perverted sex." The Ralston-Purina pullout cost NBC $1 million (Dreifus, 1992).

- Cartoonist Ralph Bakshi removed a portion of a Mighty Mouse animated cartoon when the American Family Association claimed that Mr. Mouse, who in the episode sniffs a flower, was in fact snorting cocaine (Dreifus, 1992).

- The National Coalition on Television Violence and two Christian media-monitoring groups, the American Family Association and Good News Communications, led a conference for media surveillance organizations. Their goals included establishing a Christian Film and Television Commission and "reestablishing the presence of the church in Hollywood" (Markels, 1990; Mitchell, 1990; Stevenson, 1990).

1988–1989

- Artists Space in New York lost its NEA funding, according to the NEA, because a catalog that accompanied one of its

(continued)

CENSORSHIP EFFORTS *(cont.)*

exhibits criticized the AIDS policies of elected and public figures. Some observers noted that criticism of public policies is at the heart of the democratic process (Honan, 1989).

- St. Paul, Minnesota, made it a crime to "place on public or *private* property" [italics added] any "symbol, object, appellation, characterization or graffiti" that "one knows or has reasonable grounds to know arouses anger, alarm, or resentment in others on the basis of race, color, creed, religion, or gender." On the grounds that much speech, including political speech, causes "resentment" or "alarm" in some segment of the population, the law was challenged in the Supreme Court, where it was declared unconstitutional (Greenhouse, 1992).

- Terry Rakolta campaigned against the sponsors of the TV comedy *Married . . . with Children* in efforts to have the series taken off the air. Rakolta has since become the director of Americans for Responsible Television, which lobbies TV networks and sponsors of programming it deems inappropriate for TV (Varian, 1989).

- The American Family Association, after viewing an episode of *Wiseguy* it thought too sexy for TV, persuaded advertiser General Motors to withhold advertising from future episodes that the AFA, not General Motors, deemed objectionable (Dreifus, 1992).

On a day sometime before the Impressions reading series was accused of blasphemy in California, a work by Thomas Jefferson was banned on the same grounds. On that occasion, Jefferson wrote, "Are we to have a censor whose imprimatur shall say what books may be sold, and what we may buy? . . . Whose foot is to be the measure to which ours are all to be cut or stretched? Is a priest to be our inquisitor or shall a layman simple as ourselves set up his reason as the rule. . . . It is an insult against our citizens to question whether they are rational beings or not, and [an insult] against religion to suppose it cannot stand the test of truth and reason."

Jefferson thought censorship an insult; it is also a danger. When the state, church, or private group restricts words or images from the public, the nation loses the right and gradually the ability to make up its mind about the information and entertainment it sees and hears. Historian Henry Steele Commager wrote, "Censorship . . . creates the kind of society that is incapable of exercising real discretion . . . it will create a generation incapable of appreciating the difference between independence of thought and subservience." The ideas of Jefferson and Commager are considered tenets of free societies. At least they have been the basis for the American experiment in self-rule. Yet the long list of censorship efforts belies America's belief in them. How does a people stake so much on freedom of speech and curtail that speech so often and with such zeal?

Two

THE IMAGE CAUSES THE HARM

The Great Soothing Appeal of Censorship

Censorship in the United States is offered to the public as an elixir of safety. Like the traveling salesmen whose tonics would cure what ails ya', proponents of book banning (and movie, magazine, and music banning) suggest their cure will bring an improvement in life: rid yourselves of pornography, *Catcher in the Rye,* or the *Maja Desnuda* and life will be safer, happier, more secure. Get rid of bad pictures and one is rid of bad acts. This promise of a better life, if only some magazine or movie is banished, is one reason so many people of good intentions are lured to the bonfires. The social-benefit rationale for censorship has smoothed a progressive patina over older, religious sanctions against sex. It makes the banning of books and movies seem reasonable to many Americans who would laugh at threats of brimstone and hellfire.

The most frequent advice is that sexual pictures are the root of what ails us, and so their elimination will bring an end to society's woes. Legislation and judicial rulings restricting speech in the United States target sexual material more often than any other and provide a model for campaigns against other material. Attacks against the National Endowment for the Arts (NEA) have been with few exceptions aimed at gay men and feminist women who use sexual imagery in their work. Assaults are routine against the sexual frankness in the young-adult books of Judy Blume, according to the American Library Association the most banned author in the United States. The removal of the *Maja Desnuda* from a university classroom, of Lee Friedlander's photographs from a university gallery, and of Dayton Claudio's painting from a campus art show were achieved because the works touch on sexual themes. So too does the AIDS and sex education information (which the American Library Association finds the most frequent trigger to censorship) and much of the TV programming that has come under attack, Robert Mapplethorpe's photographs, and the experimental film *Tongues Untied*. Based on the poetry of black gay men, *Tongues Untied* became a centerpiece of Patrick Buchanan's 1992 presidential bid. Buchanan assailed President Bush for allowing the NEA to support the film and hoped to build a far-right base from which to take the highest office.

In 1987 Dr. Larry Baron, a leading researcher at Yale and the University of New Hampshire on sexually explicit material, wrote a critique of Attorney General Edwin Meese's Commission on Pornography, which had recommended the restriction of sexual material. His comments might be said of much that has been censored since. "A particularly insidious aspect of the *Final Report*," wrote Baron, "is the commission's use of feminist rhetoric to attain its right-wing objectives. Replacing the outmoded cant of sin and depravity with the trendier rhetoric of harm, the commission exploited feminist outrage about sexual violence in order to bolster oppressive obscenity laws" (p. 12).

In the past five years, nonsexual material also has become a magnet of censorship efforts. Conservatives wish to restrict blasphemy and satanism, liberals wish to ban "hate speech" that they believe promotes racism, sexism, and homophobia. Yet the reasoning remains: ban the image and one is rid of the act. Image-blaming is easy to understand and peddle; it provides bumper-sticker explanations for human motive and action. It relies on the flattering notion that without invidious outside forces like rock music or film, people would be good.

The promise of benefit by banning or restricting sexual imagery is advanced by the religious far-right and the right wing of the feminist movement. (The term "right-wing feminist" is my own; others may not agree with it.) Catharine MacKinnon and Andrea Dworkin are the best-known feminist benefit-banners. MacKinnon teaches at the University of Michigan Law School and is the author of *Sexual Harassment of Working Women* (1979), *Feminism Unmodified* (1987), and *Only Words* (1993), in addition to her many contributions to law journals. Dworkin is the author of *Woman Hating* (1974), *Pornography: Men Possessing Women* (1981), *Intercourse* (1987), among other books and articles. Together they drafted a bill (1984) that redefined obscenity, currently a criminal violation, as a civil offense. Under the MacKinnon-Dworkin law, victims who believe they had been harmed by sexual material could recover monetary damages from the producers, distributors, and retailers of that material. Civil law provisions lower the standards needed to establish liability and make it easier for courts to find defendants guilty. The MacKinnon-Dworkin bill also allowed a woman—any woman, the victim of no crime—to sue producers and distributors of sexual material on behalf of all women for the material's infringement on women's civil rights. The MacKinnon-Dworkin bill, passed into law in Indianapolis, was found unconstitutional by a female Reagan-appointee trial judge and the United States Court of Appeals for the Seventh Circuit (*American Booksellers v. Hudnut*, 1985). The Appeals Court found that the law was overbroad in its inclusion of a wide range of legal materials and that it violated the *Brandenburg* standard for inciteful speech. *Brandenburg* holds that speech may be punished (and its producers and distributors sued) if it is "directed to inciting or producing imminent lawless action and . . . likely to incite or produce such action" (*Brandenburg v. Ohio*, 1969). Reviewing the MacKinnon-Dworkin bill, the court ruled that sexual material does not incite the immediate commission of illegal acts and is not likely to provoke them. The judgment was upheld by the U.S. Supreme Court (1986).

Women Against Pornography, a small but lively activist group that protests against the production and distribution of sexually explicit materials, is another key player in the feminist antipornography movement. Other antipornography groups can be found locally across the nation. Groups antecedent to Women Against Pornography included Women Against Violence Against Women and Women Against Violence and Pornography in the Media. The names suggest the shift in the feminist movement from fighting violence to attacking sexually explicit material (for a discussion of feminist antipornography politics, see Pally, 1985a; Strossen, 1993; and Taylor, in press).

The most visible of the Christian right image-blamers are Senators Jesse Helms and Strom Thurmond, along with Donald Wildmon, director of the American Family Association, Pat Robertson of the Christian Coalition, and Phyllis Schlafly of the Eagle Forum. The Christian Coalition has 750 local chapters throughout the United States, full-time staff in fifteen states, Washington lobbyists, and an annual budget of $8–$10 million (Sullivan, 1993). Robertson has raised over $13 million to support Christian Coalition candidates in electoral races (Lynn, 1993). In states such as Virginia and South Carolina, Christian Coalition members have gained control of key positions in the Republican party (Ayres Jr., 1993).

The American Family Association raised $6 million in revenues in 1990; its director Donald Wildmon earns a salary of $101,159 plus a $14,400 tax-free housing allowance (Dreifus, 1992). When *TV Guide* reported these figures, Wildmon protested that his salary was $72,500 and that the remaining $28,659 was a bonus. In the last decade, the AFA has campaigned against 137 television programs including *Let's Make a Deal, Hill Street Blues, Family Ties, Charlie's Angels, Beverly Hills 90210, The Simpsons,* and *Three's Company.* It has lobbied 139 corporations to withdraw their advertising from programming that the AFA finds offensive. Among the companies approached: American Express, American Airlines, Campbell's, Colgate-Palmolive, Dow Chemical, Dunkin' Donuts, General Motors, Hallmark,

Heinz, Kellogg's, MasterCard, Nestlé, Playtex, Revlon, Sears Roebuck, Time Inc., Toyota, and Warner Communications (Finan & Castro, 1992).

The fundamental tenet of both the Christian and the feminist right is that ridding society of sexual imagery will reduce rape, incest, and wife battery. Right-wing feminists would add sexual harassment and sexism to the list; fundamentalists would add interracial sex, homosex, and feminism. At times these political camps censure the same material, such as the more provocative fashion magazines, adult magazines (including such mainstream publications as *Playboy*), and the videos found in the adult section of one's local video store. At times, these groups do not protest jointly. Fundamentalists assail sex and AIDS education, right-wing feminists do not. The two groups may work in political coalition, as they did in 1983–84 to pass the MacKinnon-Dworkin bill in Indianapolis (Duggan, 1984). Apart from MacKinnon and Dworkin, the bill's sponsors were Mayor William Hudnut, a Presbyterian minister and conservative Republican, and Reverend Greg Dixon, a Baptist preacher and former official in the Moral Majority. These two had led the Coalition for a Clean Community on a march against immorality through Indianapolis's downtown. The final key player in the passage of the MacKinnon-Dworkin bill was Beulah Coughenour, a former Republican Councilwoman and activist in the movement to stop passage of the ERA. In 1993, Christian and feminist right-wingers supported a bill in the Massachusetts State legislature identical in all but minor detail to the 1984 law. MacKinnon testified in favor of the bill before the state's joint Judiciary Committee. Also in 1993, they favored a bill in the Senate called the Pornography Victims' Compensation Act (PVCA).

Introduced by Senator Mitch McConnell (R.-Kentucky), PVCA was intended "to provide a cause of action for victims of sexual abuse, rape, and murder, against producers and distributors of hardcore pornographic material." It required no conviction of the perpetrator and set no limit on the amount of money a publisher or distributor could be fined. Other than the subjective term "hardcore pornography," it offered no definition of what might be covered under the law. Since reasonable people disagree about which sorts of sexual material are objectionable, the bill would have allowed victims of sexual crimes to sue the publishers, distributors, exhibitors, or retailers of a wide range of legal (nonobscene) books, magazines, or movies that they believed triggered the crimes that harmed them.

PVCA distinguished itself from traditional law by holding producers and distributors liable not for the consequences of their acts but for the acts of an intervening third party. Traditional law holds individuals liable for the foreseeable effects of their acts; an intervening party breaks the chain of liability because the actions of an unknown other cannot reasonably be foreseen. PVCA held producers and distributors responsible not only for acts of a reasonable third party or common man or woman, but also for those of any mentally unbalanced person who might be triggered to commit a crime. The "most susceptible person" standard of obscenity, known as the *Hicklin* rule, has long been held unconstitutional, for it would reduce what is publicly available to what is suitable to volatile minds. Jane Whicher wrote in the *Federal Bar News & Journal* (1993),

> Imposing liability for a criminal act would mean that creators and distributors of sexually explicit materials must be aware of, and take into account, that someone might be inspired to mimic or copy some depiction in the materials they handle. That is identical to the underpinnings of the *Hicklin* rule . . . As succinctly stated by one court: "to impose liability in such circumstances would allow the freaks and misfits of society to declare what the rest of the country can and cannot read, watch, and hear" (*Watters v. TSR, Inc.*, 1990). . . . The PVCA has the anomalous result of providing greater relief for a plaintiff where there is an intervening crime than where the injury does not involve an intervening criminal act. (p. 363, 364)

Recognizing that the PVCA would be unconstitutional if it included material protected by the nation's guarantees of free speech, the Senate Judiciary Committee tried to save the bill by limiting it to illegal obscenity and child pornography. Dworkin and MacKinnon found this modification disappointing, as they wished to provide a cause of action against legal sexual material (Elson, 1992; Hentoff, 1992). Once the PVCA passed from the Judiciary Committee into the full Senate, the amendment limiting it to illegal material could have been stripped from the bill, returning it to its original form. This possibility and other objections to PVCA sparked concern and protest from booksellers, librarians, and anticensorship feminists. Feminists for Free Expression, a national nonprofit group, sent to the Senate a letter of protest signed by over 230 prominent women including Betty Friedan, Erica Jong, Adrienne Rich, Judy Blume, Susan Isaacs, Jamaica Kincaid, Nora Ephron, and Nadine Strossen (Feminists for Free Expression, 1992a).

The group wrote,

> S. 1521 [PVCA] damages crime victims by diverting attention from the substantive triggers to violence. Violence is caused by deeply-rooted economic, family, psychological and political factors, and it is these that need addressing . . . [PVCA] reinforces the "porn made me do it" excuse for rapists and batterers . . . it is book banning by bankruptcy. . . . Feminist women are especially keen to the harms of censorship, legislative or monetary. Historically, information about sex, sexual orientation, reproduction and birth control have been banned under the guise of "morality" and the "protection" of women. Such restrictions have never reduced violence.

PVCA died on the Senate floor, but not before earning the nickname "the Ted Bundy bill"—a reference to the serial killer who, when his insanity plea was denied, sought to avoid the electric chair by confessing he had committed his murders under pornography's sway.

By any moniker, PVCA is a good example of the image-blaming argument pursued by the Christian and feminist right. It proposes that pictures of sex unleash violent desire at women's bodies (if the feminists are talking) or at the body politic (if the fundamentalists). Pictures of s/m sex even more so, say feminists; images of interracial and homosex even more so, say fundamentalists. The course of the cure seems short and direct, and has the lure of peace in our time. It also has the cachet of feminist tradition. In the last twenty-five years, women and some men examined images in all sectors of Western culture, from television commercials to the films shown in medical school. This investigation became a tool for identifying sexism and exposing its pervasiveness. Sexual material deserves this scrutiny. Yet in the antipornography movement, confusion arose between examining images for their insights about society and calling those images *sources* or *causes* of social injustice (Pally, 1985a; Willis, 1981).

As the PVCA targets words and images rather than the substantive causes of violence, it bolsters none of the legal and social services that aid crime victims, such as rape crisis centers, legal counseling, or special training for police who confront domestic violence and sexual abuse. It addresses none of the underlying causes of violence such as poverty, illegal drug markets, and the sexism passed down from father to son. At bottom, the image-causes-harm idea is mistaken because it misunderstands both imagery and harm.

The mass-market pornography and rock music industries took off after World War II. Before the twentieth century, few people save a wealthy elite saw any pornography whatsoever; certainly they heard no rap or rock music. Yet violence and sexism flourished for thousands of years before the printing press and camera. Countries today where no sexual imagery or Western music is permitted, like Saudi Arabia, Iran, and China (where sale and distribution of pornography is a capital offense), do not boast social harmony and strong women's rights records (Kristof, 1991; WuDunn, 1990). Drugs have been used for centuries without rock as a guide, and in some cultures, such as Chinese and Native American, commonly by large sectors of the population. For millennia, teenagers have become pregnant without the aid of sexual imagery, rock, or matrimony. In *Intimate Matters: A History of Sexuality in America,* John D'Emilio and Estelle Freedman (1988) write that up to one-third of births in colonial America occurred out of wedlock or within eight months of hurried marriages. Homosexuals (considered a problem by the religious right) lived and coupled in every society with or without the availability of homosexual imagery.

In light of the historical success of violence and sexual and drug abuses, it is unlikely that their cause lies in the johnny-come-lately industries of pornography or rock. Banning sexually explicit material or rock is not likely to reduce those abuses or assist women and children (Burstyn, 1985). Some image-blamers argue that commercial sexual imagery has changed men's attitudes about women for the worse and so promotes violence. They cannot mean changes from those happy prepornography days when women could not vote, sign contracts, retain control of earned income or custody of their children, or appear in public without permission of fathers or husbands; when it was legal to beat one's wife with a stick; when, in Ann Snitow's concise phrase, for all but an elite of women "rape was unreportable because it was unremarkable" (1992).

Through the last decade, the media has been overfull with claims of increasing social chaos and sexual violence. The mayhem-escalation theory holds that while violence, and sexual and drug abuses have run through history, they are more rampant now as a result of sexually explicit material, rock, and rap. Yet D'Emilio and Freedman's data on out-of-wedlock births belie claims of unprecedented premarital sex. Rape rates may not be increasing, in spite of the availability of sexual images. The Bureau of Justice Statistics reports that between 1973 and 1987 the national rape rate of 0.6 per 1,000 women each year remained steady and the rate of attempted rape decreased 46 percent, from 1.3 to 0.7 per 1,000 (Associated Press, 1991b; Harlow, 1991). In 1990, the reported rape rate was 1 per 1,000 women over the age of 12, much below the rate of aggravated assault (4.5 per 1,000 women) or simple assault (12.7 per 1,000 women) (Bureau of Justice Statistics, 1992). For comparison purposes, of all crimes committed against persons, 31.7 percent involve violence, 24.9 percent assault, 68.3 percent theft, 65 percent larceny, and 0.7 percent rape (Bureau of Justice Statistics, 1992). These data on rape were gathered from household surveys rather than from police statistics, in which rapes are famously underreported. They identify at least some of the rapes that never reach police files because women believe the police will treat their complaints lightly or because they fear retaliation from the abuser, a problem frequent in cases of domestic violence. Additionally, these data cover the decades when feminists brought rape to the attention of the nation and created the social climate and community structures to encourage women to bring rape into the open. These have led to an overall increase in rape reporting. One would expect rape rates to increase, not remain steady or decrease as was found by the Bureau of Justice.

The increase in media attention to rape, including date rape and marital rape, may reflect not an increase in rape but an increase in sensitivity to it. The July 1991 issue of *Pediatrics* reports similar findings for child abuse (Feldman et al., 1991). Over the last four decades, abuse of female children has remained steady at 12 percent. These data, too, were gathered from personal surveys rather than from police files, where child abuse has been underreported. Feldman et al. attribute recent increases in child abuse reporting to the legal requirement that schools, hospitals, and other social services report child abuse to the police, and to attitudinal changes toward women and children.

These statistics are cited not to downplay the seriousness of rape and child abuse but to respect it. Those who mistakenly cry that these crimes are "worse now than ever before" suggest that such violence has to be worsening to be of note, that current rape and child abuse rates are not noteworthy enough. A 12 percent rate of child abuse is a grave social problem, as is the present incidence of rape and wife battery. A 1 percent incidence of such violence would demand remedy. Proponents of "worse now" theories leave the impression that they exploit inaccurate information as a scare tactic, not so much to aid women and children as to provide justification for conservative social policies and censorship measures the public might otherwise not tolerate.

In the decades since the 1950s, with the marketing of sexual material and rock music, the country has seen the greatest increase in sensitivity to violence against women and children. Before the pelvis-wriggler Elvis and mass publication of sexual images, no rape or incest hot lines and battered women's shelters existed; the terms *date rape* and *marital rape* were not yet in the language. Should one conclude that the presence of pornography or rock has inspired public outrage at sexual crimes? A likelier theory holds that pornography and rock do not determine the quality of life for women and children.

In a 1991 article, *New York Times* rock critic Jon Pareles examined two videotapes that attribute social harms to MTV. The first, *Rising to the Challenge,* is sold by the Parents' Music Resource Center (PMRC), the group founded by Tipper Gore that persuaded record companies to put warning labels on their product. *Rising to the Challenge* was written by Jennifer Norwood, former PMRC executive director, and Robert DeMoss, youth-culture specialist for Focus on the Family, a Christian fundamentalist group. The second tape, *Dreamworlds,* was made by Sut Jhally, professor of communications at the University of Massachusetts, and is being sold for classroom use.

Upon investigating *Rising to the Challenge,* Pareles discovered that the violent incidents allegedly inspired by certain rock videos occurred before most of these videos were released, "suggesting that the music reflects the culture instead of driving it." On examining *Dreamworlds,* Pareles found that the images of women were ripped out of context—Jhally failed to indicate what proportion they form of all music video images or even what videos they came from. Viewing long passages of MTV as they were broadcast, Pareles found approximately one in six clips with "ornamental" or "sexy" women and "two minutes per hour of female bimbofication, along with such various nonbimbos as moms, teachers, old women and children." Music videos also include female singers and bands. Pareles concluded with this observation: "When a teenager sees some guy with waist-length two-tone hair, wearing leopard-print spandex and studded leather standing in a spotlight holding a guitar, he or she can probably figure out that it's a performance, a show, a fantasy— part of a privileged arena far away from daily life. Given the evidence, I wish I could say the same about their elders" (Pareles, 1991).

Three

STANDARD DEVIATION
Research Literature on Sexually Explicit Material and Social Harms

Between 1968 and 1970, the U.S. Commission on Obscenity and Pornography (also known as the President's Commission) studied the relationship between sexually explicit material and antisocial behavior. Over this two-year period, it conducted controlled laboratory studies and national surveys on pornography consumption and crimes rates. The budget of $2 million in 1970 dollars exceeded by several times the $500,000 in 1985 dollars allotted Attorney General Meese's Commission on Pornography. Below are a few of the President's commission's concluding remarks:

> "Empirical research designed to clarify the question has found no
> reliable evidence to date that exposure to explicit sexual ma-
> terials plays a significant role in the causation of delinquent

or criminal sexual behavior among youths or adults" (U.S. Commission on Obscenity and Pornography, 1970, p. 139).

"Studies of juvenile delinquents indicate that their experience with erotica is generally similar to that of nondelinquents. . . . There is no basis in the available data however for supposing that there is any independent relationship between exposure to erotica and delinquency" (p. 242).

"If a case is to be made against pornography in 1970, it will have to be made on grounds other than demonstrated effects of a damaging personal or social nature" (p. 139).

Two members of the U.S. Commission wrote at the time, "We would have welcomed evidence relating exposure to erotica to delinquency, crime and anti-social behavior, for if any such evidence existed we might have a simple solution to some of our most urgent problems. However, the research fails to establish a meaningful causal relationship or even significant correlation between exposure to erotica and immediate or delayed anti-social behavior among adults. To assert the contrary . . . is not only to deny the facts, but also to delude the public by offering a spurious and simplistic answer to highly complex problems" (Fleishman, 1972).

In the years since 1970, two notions have become popular: first, that pornography has become more violent and more widespread; second, that as a result, it is responsible for antisocial behavior, specifically sexual perversions and violence against women and children. In 1985, Attorney General Edwin Meese authorized another commission to study the social and psychological effects of sexually explicit material. The publicity surrounding the commission led to the belief that the pornography-causes-harm hypothesis was confirmed, yet the commission's investigation of the science did not support this conclusion. University of Michigan law professor Dr. Frederick Schauer (1987), a member of the Meese Commission, authored a draft document that served as a basis for the commission's report. He wrote,

I do not make the claim, nor does the Report, that the category of sexually explicit material bears a causal relationship to acts of sexual violence. I do not make the claim, nor does the Report, that the degree of explicitness is relevant in explaining the causal relationship between depictions of sexual violence and acts of sexual violence. . . . As the evidence so clearly indicates, and as the Report so clearly, and in italics, states, the causal relationship is independent of the degree of sexual explicitness. . . . The Report itself never even hints at expanding the area of permissible regulation beyond that permitted by *Miller* [the current standard for judging obscene materials] and its associated cases. . . . Although I can appreciate symbolic reasons for regulating the tiny sliver of the sexually violent market that is obscene . . . I can appreciate as well that the marginal symbolic advantages . . . would not outweigh the costs. Thus I do not find the possibility of total deregulation troublesome, and I never have (pp. 767–768).

In interviews at the close of the commission's investigations, Dr. Park Dietz, a Meese Commission member and medical director of the Institute of Law, Psychiatry and Public Policy at the University of Virginia, said, "*Playboy* centerfolds are in a category that the commission says is harmless, and that I personally think is actually healthy in many respects" (Ferraro, 1986). His views were echoed by Henry Hudson, chairman of the commission, who said, "A lot of critics think that our report focuses on publications like *Playboy* and *Penthouse* and that is totally untrue" (MacNeil/Lehrer, 1986).

Since the 1970 commission, and especially since the mid-'80s, when image-blaming theories made pornography research legitimate grounds for tenure, the social sciences have produced a sizable literature on the study of sexual material. The findings are limited by certain methodological problems, most important: generalizing from the laboratory to life; the sexual bravado effect on the questionnaire responses of college males (the most common subjects of research experiments on sexual imagery); the "experimenter demand effect" that causes subjects to guess, however unconsciously, at the experimenter's hypothesis and try to fulfill it; and the implausibility of all studies involving electrical "shocks" (subjects in laboratory experiments understand that researchers cannot allow participants to be hurt).

METHODOLOGICAL ISSUES IN SOCIAL SCIENCE RESEARCH

- In their writings, Drs. Neil Malamuth (University of California), David Shore (Southern Illinois University), Edward Donnerstein (University of California), and Daniel Linz (University of California) have noted that the Meese Commission failed to take into account certain important methodological problems that confound all social science data. Donnerstein and Linz (1986) wrote, "Some commission members apparently did not understand or chose not to heed some of the fundamental assumptions in the social science research on pornography" (p. 56).

- The 1986 Surgeon General's Workshop on pornography devoted eight pages of its report to the methodological problems running through the scientific literature. Chief among the data's limitations are (Surgeon General's Workshop on Pornography and Public Health, 1986, pp. 5–13):

1. Results achieved in the experimental laboratory are notoriously bad predictors of behavior outside the lab. The Surgeon General's Workshop concluded, "The drawback of such a [laboratory] approach is its inherent artificiality; phenomena in the lab are not always what they may be in the real world";

2. Self-reporting questionnaires (which pose questions, for instance, about one's willingness to use force for sex) are poor indicators of real-life behavior. People exaggerate or minimize, and often do not do what they say;

3. Experiments in which subjects are asked to hurt a confederate "subject" are also poor predictors of real-life behavior as participants are likely to know that researchers

would not allow their subjects to be hurt. In 1986, David Shore, editor of the *Journal of Social Work & Human Sexuality*, wrote, "Some recent works have suggested violence in pornography elevates aggression. . . . It should be noted that my research has lead to my concurring with Katchadourian that 'the experimental situations set up in these studies tend to be contrived, and the tests used artificial, [thus] their significance with respect to deviant behaviors remains uncertain'";

4. Researchers are inclined to interpret events according to their own beliefs, especially those reporting on field studies, in which the intricacy of real-world settings leaves room for a range of constructions. "The most subtle problem with clinical reports," noted the Surgeon General's Workshop, "is the inevitable tendency . . . to interpret and report their observations in a way that supports their beliefs" (Surgeon General, 1986, p. 8);

5. Only successful studies are reported in the literature. "As a result," wrote the Surgeon General's workshop, "it is difficult to know how many studies were done that were unable to produce any observed result . . . the presence of a large number of these unreported results may indicate that the regularity and strength of a particular effect is really rather low even though it has been reported to have occurred under controlled conditions" (Surgeon General, 1986, p. 10);

6. Correlational data do not establish causality. The number of drownings per day correlates highly with the sales of sunglasses, but it would be a mistake to say sun glasses cause drownings, or vice versa (Surgeon General, 1986, p. 11);

7. Clinical studies of convicted sex offenders cannot separate their use of pornography from other highly significant factors that promote violence, such as drug or alcohol abuse,

(continued)

METHODOLOGICAL ISSUES *(cont.)*

poverty, and abusive childhoods. "Clinical studies are limited in value," wrote the Surgeon General's Workshop. "Their greatest limitation is the inability to isolate the specific effects of the variable being considered (such as exposure to pornography) from other potentially influential variables" (Surgeon General, 1986, p. 7);

8. "Clinical studies have another problem resulting from their focus only on youth with identified problems. The effects of . . . sexual abuse cannot be separated accurately from the effects of the discovery of those circumstances. For instance, it is impossible to tell with any rigor how much of the distress shown by a child in therapy results from actual participation in pornography and how much is precipitated by the reactions of others such as parents, friends, and teachers to the discovery of the child's involvement. For example, Burgess et al. (1984) found that behavioral problems of some children involved in sex and pornography rings increased after their participation was discovered" (Surgeon General, 1986, p. 7);

9. The "desensitization" reported with repeated viewing of sexual material may be the boredom that results from repeatedly viewing any sort of material. During hearings of the Attorney General's Commission, Donnerstein pointed out that emergency room doctors do not faint at each new wounded body, yet they also do not take to the streets and commit murder;

10. Most of the research on pornography has been conducted on college men—a group especially vulnerable to the sexual bravado effect. Does a subject's knowledge that his answers will be compared to those of other college men skew his responses?

11. All laboratory experiments are subject to the "experimenter demand" effect, in which subjects unconsciously

try to guess at the experimenter's hypothesis and to confirm it.

• In their review of literature on pornography for the British Home Office Research and Planning Unit, Drs. Dennis Howitt and Guy Cumberbatch (1990) also note problems in research methodology, most notably,

It should not be forgotten that social science research, as well as the pornography debate, takes places in a broad ideological climate which may influence how research is done, what research is done, and what is said about the research. . . . Thus while the laboratory-based researchers (such as Donnerstein, Byrne, Zillmann) are often assumed to provide the strongest evidence concerning the causal effects of pornography on behaviour, the literature reveals that this research is quite controversial. . . . A great many studies (especially those involving experimental laboratory methods) are based on North American university students who often participate in the research in order to obtain credits towards their degrees. Indeed, most of the studies are confined to a very small range of universities so that sometimes students at Wisconsin University taking a particular course have supplied all of the available evidence for a particular point of view. (pp. 85, 89)

VIOLENCE IN SEXUALLY EXPLICIT IMAGERY

To arrive at its recommendations to restrict sexually explicit material, the Attorney General's Commission concluded that (1) pornography has become more violent since the 1970 U.S. Commission on Pornography, which found no link between sexual material and antisocial behavior and recommended no restrictions; (2) pornographic images so significantly change men's attitudes about women that they promote and foster sexual assault. Yet, the notion that sexually explicit material has become more violent is not supported by the evidence.

In their analysis of 4,644 "pornographic" magazines, Attorney General Edwin Meese's Commission on Pornography concluded that publications such as *Playboy*, *Penthouse* and *Playgirl* should not be considered pornographic. Dr. Jennings Bryant, whose research was heavily cited by the Meese Commission to condemn sexually explicit material, classified *Penthouse*, *Playboy,* and *Playgirl,* as "R-rated softcore sexually oriented magazines" (Attorney General's Commission, 1986).Reviewing the literature on violence in sexually explicit material, Donnerstein and Linz (1986) wrote, "We cannot legitimately conclude that pornography has become more violent since the time of the 1970 Pornography Commission" (p. 57). In 1987, Linz, Donnerstein, and Penrod repeated their findings in an *American Psychologist* article: "The available data might suggest that there has actually been a decline in violent images within mainstream publications such as *Playboy* and that comparisons of 'X' rated materials with other depictions suggests there is in fact far more violence in the *non*pornographic fare."

Dr. Joseph Scott and Steven Cuvelier (1987a, 1987b), both of Ohio State University, ran a content analysis of *Playboy* over a thirty-year period and found an average of *1.89* violent pictorials per year, with violence decreasing through the '80s. They wrote (1987b), "Although the overall number and ratio of violent cartoons and pictorials in *Playboy* over the 30-year period examined was rare, a major question addressed was whether the amount of violence was increasing. Rather than a linear relation, a curvilinear relationship was observed with the amount of violence on the decrease. . . . Those who argue for greater censorship of magazines such as *Playboy* because of its depictions of violence need a new rationale to justify their position" (p. 279). In concluding their findings for the *Journal of Sex Research*, Scott and Cuvelier (1987a) wrote, "In the oldest continuously published adult magazine in the U.S., the number of sexually violent depictions has always been extremely small and the number of such depictions has decreased in recent years" (p. 538).

In her study of commercial, sexually explicit films directed by men and women, Dr. Patti Britton (1993a) found that "fewer than 1 percent of pseudoviolent or coercive acts were portrayed overall, with a mean designation of 0.55 such acts for the female directors and 0.75 for the male directors." Dr. Ted Palys (1986) of Simon Fraser University came to similar findings in his study of sexually explicit (XXX) video cassettes. He reported a decrease in violence in sexually explicit videos between the 1970s and mid-1980s. More violence was found in videos without explicit sexual activity than in the triple-X variety. In a 1990 content analysis of current videotapes, Drs. Ni Yang and Daniel Linz (University of California) found that in XXX explicit pornography, sex accounted for 41 percent of all behavioral sequences, sexual violence for 4.73 percent, and nonsexual violence again for 4.73 percent. In R-rated films, sexual behavior accounted for 4.59 percent of all sequences, sexual violence accounted for 3.27 percent, and nonsexual violence for 35 percent.

SEXUAL IMAGERY AND AGGRESSION

The research refuting the claim that sexual imagery triggers aggression has exhausted volumes far longer than this one. A thorough overview can be read in *The Question of Pornography: Research Findings and Policy Implications*, in which authors Donnerstein, Linz, and Penrod (1987) conclude, "Should harsher penalties be leveled against persons who traffic in pornography, particularly violent pornography? We do not believe so. Rather, it is our opinion that the most prudent course of action would be the development of educational programs that would teach viewers to become more critical consumers of the mass media. . . . Educational programs and stricter obscenity laws are not mutually exclusive, but the legal course of action is more restrictive of personal freedoms than an educational approach. And, as we have noted, the existing research probably does not justify this approach" (p. 172).

In 1993, the National Research Council's Panel on Understanding and Preventing Violence (Reiss & Roth, 1993) wrote, "Demonstrated empirical links between pornography and sex crimes in general are weak or absent. Studies of individual sex offenders have found no link between their offenses and their use of pornography; if anything, they do not appear to use pornography as much as the average male" (p. 111). During the year of its investigations, the Attorney General's Commission asked Dr. Edna Einsiedel (University of Calgary) to write an independent review of the social science literature. Her report again found no link between sexually explicit material and sex crimes. "Unfortunately," wrote Dr. Larry Baron (1987), "the commission paid little attention to the excellent review of the empirical literature that was prepared by the staff social scientist, Edna Einsiedel. . . . It would be instructive for those unfamiliar with the research on pornography to read Einsiedel's comprehensive literature review and then read [Commissioner Frederick] Schauer's deceptive executive summary" (p. 8).

After Einsiedel submitted her unwanted report to the Attorney General's Commission, the commissioners asked then Surgeon General C. E. Koop to gather additional data. Koop conducted a conference of researchers and practitioners in the medical and social science fields. His report once again found no link between sexual material and violence (Surgeon General's Workshop, 1986). "Pornography has been consistently linked to changes in some perceptions, attitudes and behaviors. These links, however, are circumscribed, few in number, and generally laboratory-based. . . . For instance, while it is a common belief that attitude changes lead to behavioral changes, research has consistently shown otherwise. Behaviors are as likely to influence attitudes as attitudes are to influence behavior" (p. 35).

The Surgeon General's Workshop came to five conclusions about sexually explicit material that the research supports "with confidence," none pointing to a substantive link between sexually explicit material and crime.

1. Children and adolescents who participate in the production of pornography experience adverse effects (p. 13). In remedy, the conference called for "innovative programs to address

the particular needs of a broad group of disenfranchised youth. . . . The reality of the situation is that someone has to go onto the street and establish programs that appeal to the youth there" (p. 55).

2. "Prolonged use of pornography increases belief that less common sexual practices are more common" (p. 17). The report concluded, "The estimates [of the frequency of varied sexual practices] of the intermediate and massive exposure [to pornography] groups were actually more accurate than the no exposure group, which underestimated the prevalence of these behaviors" (p. 17).

3. Pornography that portrays sexual aggression as pleasurable for the victim increases the acceptance of the use of coercion in sexual relations within the lab setting (p. 19). "It is important to remain aware, however, that the observed attitude changes are generally restricted to exposure using depictions of sexually violent incidents in which the victim becomes aroused as a result of the attack. Attitude changes from exposure to violence or sexually explicit behavior alone are not consistently observed" (p. 22).

4. "Acceptance of coercive sexuality appears to be related to sexual aggression. . . . The association between attitudes and behavior in this area is one of the most difficult to comment upon conclusively. . . . It cannot be said presently that these attitudes are causally related to this [sexually aggressive] behavior. Moreover, it is not clear that exposure to pornography is the most significant factor in the development of these attitudes" (p. 23).

"An unresolved issue is whether these attitudes led to different [abusive] behavior patterns or whether the attitudes were adopted after the subject's behavior patterns were already established" (p. 25).

One study published just prior to the Surgeon General's Workshop report investigated attitudes about women and real-world aggression (Ageton, 1983). It found that involvement in a delinquent peer group appeared consistently as the most powerful factor prompting aggression, accounting for 76 percent of sexual violence. Three other factors, including attitudes about women and violence, accounted altogether for 19 percent of aggression (p. 119; see also Surgeon General's Workshop, 1986, p. 27).

5. "In laboratory studies . . . exposure to violent pornography increases punitive behavior toward women. An increase in aggressive behavior toward women has been proposed often as one likely effect of exposure to pornography but there does not seem to be sufficient scientific support for a generalized statement regarding the presence of this effect" (Surgeon General's Workshop, 1986, pp. 28–29).

"Reports of this causal relationship being a noticeable one in the real world have not emerged consistently. In sum these experiments should heighten concern that aggressive behavior toward women may be increased by viewing aggressive and sexually aggressive films, but presently this effect has only been seen in controlled and potentially artificial laboratory settings" (p. 34).

Disregarding the Einsiedel and Surgeon General reports equally, Attorney General Meese's Commission recommended that government restrict sexually explicit material. Two commissioners, Dr. Judith Becker and Ellen Levine, so disagreed with the recommendations that they issued a dissenting report (1986). Lambasting the commission for a "paucity of certain types of testimony including dissenting expert opinion," they concluded, "No self-respecting investigator would accept conclusions based on such a study" (p. 4, 7). Dr. Becker, then director of the Sexual Behavior Clinic at New York State Psychiatric Institute, told *The New York Times,* "I've been working with sex offenders for 10 years and have reviewed the scientific literature, and I don't think a causal link exists between pornography and sex crimes" (Goleman, 1986).

Dr. Edward Donnerstein called the commission's conclusions "bizarre" (Goleman, 1986). He and other researchers such as Drs. Neil Malamuth and Daniel Linz found no change in acts or attitudes toward women when men were shown nonviolent sexual images that comprise the bulk of the pornography market. Summarizing their views, Donnerstein and Linz (1986) wrote, "We feel it necessary to point out that the report fell short of our expectations in several important respects. First there are factual problems. . . . Several of the contentions made in its pages cannot be supported by empirical evidence" (p. 56).

In the same month as the Meese Commission completed its hearings, Dr. David Shore (1986), editor of the *Journal of Social Work & Human Sexuality*, wrote,

> There is no current validity to the hypothesis that the extent of exposure to erotica is positively associated with the immediate or later emergence of sexual pathology in general, and pedophilia in particular. My conclusions are consistent with those of Dr. Herant Katchadourian, the highly respected Stanford University physician who undertook a similar review of the literature for the 4th edition of his widely adopted textbook *Fundamentals of Human Sexuality*. . . . Moreover, child molesters were found to be essentially unmoved by such stimulation. . . . From a cross cultural perspective, the Danish experience with the legalization of pornography and the Japanese experience with open aggressive erotica at the very least suggest that erotica does not increase the prevalence of sex crimes.

A year after the Attorney General's Commission released its final report, Linz, Donnerstein, and Penrod (1987) tried again to dispel the commission's misreporting of the evidence. "To single out pornography for more stringent legal action is inappropriate—based on the empirical research. . . . If the Commissioners were looking for ways to curb the most nefarious media threat to public safety, they missed it" (p. 29). Their efforts were supported by Dr. Larry Baron (1987) who wrote in *Society*, "There is no empirical evidence to support the conclusion that nonviolent pornography increases aggression against women" (p. 9).

Two years later, Donnerstein was called by the Ontario District Court in *Her Majesty against Fringe Product, Inc.* (1989) to address the relation between images and antisocial crimes.

Q: Can you predict what phenomena will set these predis-posed, already aggressive individuals off?

A: I wish we could. . . . Certain people are influenced by who knows what. If you find a serial murderer and he's modeled something he sees, it could be any type of material. We know full well, with pedophiles, they are just as turned on by child pornog-raphy, which is obviously illegal, [as by] a picture of a young male or female in the Sears catalogue in underwear. It is very difficult to say what type of stimuli are going to take those individuals on the fringe, predisposed, and cause them to act in a certain way. (p. 205)

In November of the following year, before the Indecent Publica-tions Tribunal of New Zealand (1990), Donnerstein commented again on the idea that sexually explicit materials act as a trigger to sexual aggression. He was "of the view that the vast majority of studies indicated that no such trigger mechanism or capacity ex-isted" (p. 11). At the same hearings, Daniel Linz testified, "With respect to case studies, it has not been established if the materials presented caused that person to be violent, or that an already violent individual is drawn to violent materials that reaffirm existing atti-tudes or predispositions. In fact, many studies have found that fol-lowing prolonged exposure to extremely sexually exciting stimuli, there are lowered levels of aggression, and there is the corollary that the individual with less exposure actually behaves in a more violent fashion than the person with more exposure" (p. 17).

The government of New Zealand also invited Dr. John Court (Fuller Theological Seminary, Pasadena, Ca.) to testify at its hearings on sexually explicit material. In previous articles and testimony, Court had reported finding a causal relationship between sexually explicit materials and sex crimes. Yet, when asked directly at the New Zealand tribunal, Court presented his views this way:

Q: Do you say that there is no causal link between nonviolent erotica and sexual crimes?

A: No, I don't say that. . . . What I am saying is that we do not have evidence that there is such a causal link. I cannot sustain it from my data and I don't know anybody who can. (pp. 14–15).

Along with their testimony at the New Zealand hearings, Donnerstein and Linz (1990) prepared a written overview of the science literature for the New Zealand government. "Despite the Attorney General's Commission assertion that most forms of pornography have a causal relationship to sexually aggressive behavior," they wrote, "we find it difficult to understand how this conclusion was reached. . . . most social scientists who testified before the Commission were also cautious, even when making statements about causal links between exposure to *violent* pornography [emphasis original] and sexually aggressive behavior. Any reasonable review of the research literature would not come to the conclusion reached by the Attorney General's Commission that pornography conclusively results in anti-social effects" (p. 6). They continued, "Studies in which individuals have been massively exposed to this [*Penthouse*] type of material have shown either reductions in laboratory aggression or no increases in aggressive behavior. Consequently, the conclusion that nonviolent degrading materials influence sexual aggression is without support" (p. 41).

"DEGRADING" OR "KINKY" SEXUAL MATERIAL AND AGGRESSION

Having found no substantive evidence of negative effects from exposure to nonviolent sexual material, researchers investigated material that is "kinky" (nonnormative), or "degrading," that is, which depicts women in subordinate positions. This research is rife with problems of definition. Is a woman inviting intercourse subordinate, in love, or commanding? Is oral or anal sex "normal"? Researchers proceeded in their investigations with their idea of nonnormative sexual images and found no link between "degrading" or "kinky" pornography and aggression against women (Zillmann & Bryant, 1984). Several found that viewing sexual material produced a decrease in aggression in male subjects. (Baron, R., 1974a; Baron, R., 1974b; Baron, R., 1977; Baron, R. & Bell, 1973, 1977; Malamuth, 1978a; White, 1979; Zillmann, 1979; Zillmann & Bryant, 1982). In one study, Zillmann and Bryant (1982) found an increase in callous attitudes toward women after subjects were exposed to "degrading" sexual material. Other researchers have not been able to replicate this component of the Zillmann and Bryant research.

In 1987, *American Psychologist* reported, "Only one study has shown that long-term exposure to this type of [degrading] material changes an individual's perception of a rape victim (Zillmann & Bryant, 1982). But later studies with both male and female viewers have not replicated these findings (Krafka, 1985; Linz, 1985). Furthermore, only one study has found changes in subjects' willingness to say they would use force with a woman in order to have sex. This study, conducted by Check (1984), involved several methodological procedures which prevent us from placing as much confidence in the outcome as we would like" (Linz, Donnerstein, & Penrod, 1987). The Check research was prepared for the Canadian government's 1984 review of sexually explicit material and was so severely flawed the government rejected it.

In his 1989 testimony to the District Court of Ontario (*Her Majesty*, 1989), Donnerstein was asked, "As to the existence of negative effects arising from dehumanizing or degrading and sexually explicit material, what is the bottom line on that?" Donnerstein said, "There is too much conflicting data, too much controversy, too much methodological problems to make a statement. . . . I would have to lean, however . . . that there are no effects or if effects occur at all, just like with violent material, they can in fact occur . . . outside the context of sexual explicitness" (p. 172). The following year, at the New Zealand hearings, Donnerstein testified that a review of the research would not conclude that exposure to "degrading" pornography yields antisocial behavior. "Finally," he said (Indecent Publications Tribunal, 1990), "specific depictions of the anal region do not seem to indicate any changes in specific attitudes about women or acceptability of violence against women" (p. 12). He added that he "knew of no research which suggested that men with a sexual interest in adult women with shaved genitals had therefore an interest in children (p. 12)."

As before, neither the Surgeon General's Workshop on pornography nor the Einsiedel review of the scientific literature for the Attorney General's Commission found a link between "degrading" pornography and sex crimes or aggression. Einsiedel concluded that the data on "degrading" pornography was too methodologically confused to use (Attorney General's Commission, 1986). The Surgeon General's Workshop found only the following statement about "degrading" sexual imagery to be reliable: that exposure to such imagery caused subjects to think that a wider variety of sexual practices were commonly done. Exposure causes subjects to estimate the prevalence of varied sexual practices *more accurately* (p. 17).

In addition to probing the link between aggression and "kinky" or "degrading" material, researchers have investigated the effects of such material on women's self-esteem, attitudes about pre- and extra-marital sex, and family stability. Dr. Carol Krafka found that women exposed to sexually degrading materials did not engage in more sex role stereotyping, experience lower self-esteem, less satisfaction with body image, more negative beliefs about rape, or show greater acceptance of violence against women (Krafka, 1985). Donnerstein came to similar results in a 1984 study; Linz, Donnerstein, and Penrod again in 1988.

Drs. Dolf Zillmann and Jennings Bryant (1984, 1989; Surgeon General's Workshop, 1986) found that exposure to pornography produced more acceptance of premarital and extramarital sexual relations, less satisfaction with one's sexual partner, and less emphasis on marriage and having children. Other researchers have questioned Zillmann and Bryant's focus on sexually explicit material, noting that varying opinions about sex and family life are found frequently in nonexplicit fare. In their 1990 overview of the literature, Donnerstein and Linz ask, "What if these ideas [about premarital sex, marriage, and children] had been presented in a nonsexually explicit format, would the effects have remained the same? . . . [These ideas] are not endemic to pornography nor are they unavailable in other forms of mass media entertainment . . . findings such as those claimed by Zillmann and Bryant must remain tentative" (p. 33).

VIOLENT SEXUAL MATERIAL AND AGGRESSION

The research on sexually violent images is the most inconsistent of the social science literature. Donnerstein, Linz, Penrod and Berkowitz found that exposure to violent imagery—sexual or nonsexual—increased aggression toward women in the laboratory context (Donnerstein, 1983; Donnerstein, 1984; Donnerstein & Berkowitz, 1981; Donnerstein & Linz, 1986; Donnerstein, Linz, & Penrod, 1987; Linz, Donnerstein, & Penrod, 1984, 1988; Wilson, Linz, & Randall, 1990). Drs. Neil Malamuth and Joseph Ceniti did not (Malamuth & Ceniti, 1986). Donnerstein and Linz attribute the aggressive effects in their experiments to the violent content of images rather than sexual content. When they and other researchers showed subjects sexual imagery with no violence, they saw no aggressive effects. When they showed subjects violent imagery with no sex, they saw the most aggressive results. In *Psychology Today* Donnerstein and Linz wrote (1986), "The most callous attitudes about rape . . . were found among those men who had seen only the violent coercion. Subjects who saw the X-rated version without violence scored lowest" (p. 59).

However unfortunate, this research predicts poorly the antecedant conditions of violence in life. In testimony to the District Court of Ontario (*Her Majesty*, 1989), Edward Donnerstein identified perhaps the most damaging evidence against his and other researchers' laboratory studies on violence. Any form of physical arousal, including exercise, will increase aggressiveness in the lab. "The measure," Donnerstein said, "is simply arousal, not sexual arousal. The Zillmann research strongly shows that once you get arousal up—the measures could be heart rate, galvanic skin response, blood pressure is the common one—if arousal is high and subjects are aggressing, it's going to facilitate aggressive behavior, independent of where the arousal is coming from. And yes, there are studies where males bicycle ride and then are more aggressive when they are angered" (p. 303).

To sum up this research, subjects in laboratory experiments will aggress if they are angered. If they are additionally "worked up" or aroused in any way, their aggression will increase. These results are not limited to viewing sexual or violent imagery and will occur if men exercise with aerobics. Finally, all responses in a laboratory setting will increase after subjects are worked up by aerobics or film viewing—not only responses of aggression against women but responses of kindness and generosity (Zillmann, 1984).

In a 1978 study, Malamuth found that college-aged men in lab experiments showed increased aggression toward female confederate "subjects" after viewing sexually violent material if the men were told it was permissible to aggress against the women. When they were given no encouragement to aggress, they did not (Malamuth, 1978b). Malamuth's findings pose significant problems for the laboratory research on violent imagery, as the experimental setup often conveys permission to aggress. The most common experimental design offers subjects the opportunity to give [mock] electric shocks to a confederate of the experiment, but does not provide them with opportunities to respond in neutral or positive ways. The "experimenter demand" affect, where subjects unconsciously try to fulfill the researchers' premise, aggravates methodological problems, as does the subjects' knowledge that it would violate research ethics to have them administer real shocks. In her paper to the American Sociological Association, Madeline Morris (1985) (Yale University) noted another deficiency of the research on violent imagery. "This finding has been interpreted by some to mean that violent pornography fosters sexual aggression against women. Such an interpretation is inappropriate since nonsexual aggression [mock electric shocks] is not a valid indicator of sexual aggression" (p. 23).

In 1990, Donnerstein and Linz wrote this warning about their own research on violent imagery as well as that of others: "The Commission states there is a 'causal relationship' between exposure to sexually violent materials and aggression toward women. This is an accurate statement, as long as we are referring to laboratory studies of aggression. . . . Whether this aggression, usually in the form of delivering [mock] electric shocks, is representative of real world aggression, such as rape, is entirely a different matter" (pp. 37–38).

After the release of the Attorney General's Report on Pornography, Malamuth wrote a letter to *American Psychologist* (*Her Majesty*, 1989) to correct misstatements published there about material that "portrays sexual aggression as pleasurable for the victim." He wrote, "We [the Surgeon General's Workshop] did not reach the consensus that 'this type of pornography is at the root of much of the rape that occurs today' . . . We also agreed that 'acceptance of coercive sexuality appears to be related to sexual aggression,' but we did not conclude that 'if a man sees a steady stream of sexually violent material . . . he begins to believe that coercion and violence are acceptable . . . and may himself become the perpetrator'" (p. 180). Malamuth's statements suggest that "acceptance of coercive sexuality" comes not from a stream of violent material but from other sources in the individual's past such as family or peer group conduct.

In their review of the literature for the British government, Howitt and Cumberbatch (1990) echo the reservations of Donnerstein, Linz, and Malamuth regarding the research on sexually violent material. They wrote in *Pornography: Impacts and Influences*,

> It is frequently argued by some laboratory researchers that pornography showing coercive and extreme sexual violence (as opposed to simply explicit erotic material) is more likely to increase aggression against women. The evidence for this is far more limited than is ideal for purposes of drawing conclusions, being based on a few but highly similar studies. It is, consequently, difficult to accept that a relationship has been firmly established in the laboratory. Moreover, given the serious problems in generalising from phenomena observed in the laboratory to the real world, it would seem highly dubious to claim that such materials are responsible for real-life effects. While the evidence is very limited, field studies and longer-term studies tend to suggest little or no effects compared with the short-term laboratory experiments (p. 84).

Drs. Howard Barbaree and William Marshall (Queen's College, Kingston Ontario) found in 1991 that "For most men, hearing a description of an encounter where the man is forcing the woman to have sex, and the woman is in distress or pain, dampens the arousal by about 50 percent compared to arousal levels using a scene of consenting lovemaking. . . . Ordinarily violence inhibits sexual arousal in men. A blood flow loss of 50 percent means a man would not be able to penetrate a woman" (Barbaree & Marshall, 1991; Goleman, 1991a).

Drs. Suzanne Ageton, Judith Becker, and Robert Stein are among the few scientists to investigate exposure to sexual materials, attitudes about women, and aggression in life situations. As reported above, Ageton (1983) found that involvement in a delinquent peer group appeared consistently as the most powerful factor in determining violence, accounting for 76 percent of sexual aggression. All other factors, including attitudes about women and violence, accounted altogether for 19 percent of aggression. In their study on sex crimes committed by adolescents, Becker and Stein (1991) found that, as with adults, sex crimes were linked to sexual and physical abuse in the perpetrator's childhood and to alcohol consumption rather than to exposure to sexually explicit material. Dr. Becker wrote, "Those offenders who consumed alcohol had a higher number of victims than those who did not and those who reported that alcohol increased their arousal had the most victims; those offenders who had been sexually abused had more victims than offenders with no history of sexual victimization; those offenders who had been physically abused had more victims than those with no history of physical abuse . . . only two subjects reported (10 percent) that sexually explicit material could have possibly played a role in their commission of a sexual crime. None of the subjects reported viewing a sexually explicit video that contained violent or deviant sexual activity" (pp. 93–94).

Becker and Stein came to these results though it was in the interest of their subjects to blame outside influences such as pornography for their crimes. "[V]ery often the self-report of sex offenders can be self-serving," the authors wrote, "and consequently one would hypothesize that offenders might be inclined to implicate sexually explicit material as a factor in the commission of the crime" (p. 94).

Psychologist Victor Cline offers the provocative theory of pornography addiction to explain the link he believes exists between sexually explicit material and violence. Sexually explicit material, according to Cline, creates a cumulative effect, leading the viewer to need more hard-core or violent fare, which in turn leads to violent behavior. Whatever the merits of his theory, they have not been tested by laboratory or field research, crime surveys, or analysis of law enforcement statistics. Dr. Elizabeth Allgeier, editor of the *Journal of Sex Research*, reported (1991) that Cline has conducted no empirical studies and published no scholarly articles on sexual material. He has three articles on the effects of television violence on children in such popular publications as *Ladies' Home Journal* (1975) and *Life* magazine (1970), and one article on the effects of television violence on children in a professional publication (Cline, 1973). He has edited one book, *Where Do You Draw the Line?* (1974) for Brigham Young University Press, a Mormon publishing house. In the 1990 *Sexual Interactions*, which reviews all research in the field, the authors did not include or mention work by Cline (Allgeier, 1990).

Einsiedel, in her review of the science for Attorney General Meese's Commission, reported that there is no evidence that exposure to hard-core, violent, or paraphiliac pornography creates an attraction to such material or stimulates a need for it, as Cline suggests (Attorney General's Commission, 1986). She noted the study by Zillmann (1984) which allowed male college students to choose to watch an X or XXX videotape. Many chose the XXX tape, which included some paraphiliac material depicting "nonnormative" sexual acts. Einsiedel called this choice a "curiosity. There is no evidence in the Zillmann study that the students liked the paraphilias or developed a taste for them" (Attorney General's Commission, 1986). Donnerstein and Linz also found that repeated exposure to sexually explicit material does not establish an addiction for it (Donnerstein & Linz, 1986).

The research of Einsiedel, Donnerstein, and Linz is supported by data gathered by the FBI. In a 1993 interview, FBI Agent Ken Lanning said, "The FBI has no evidence that pornography causes crimes. Eighty-one percent of the killers in the FBI study on violent crimes said they had a sexual interest in pornography, but I'm not sure if we took 100 regular guys we wouldn't find the same thing. Pornography might be a catalyst, but many things can be catalysts. I interviewed a child killer who told me the greatest influence on his fantasy life was *Tom Sawyer.*" In the FBI's four-year study on serial killers, pornography is discussed only as corroborative evidence needed to get a search warrant and, when the material fits the legal definition of obscenity, as a violation of obscenity laws (Ressler, Burgess, & Douglas, 1988). Dr. Ann Burgess, one of the authors of the FBI study on violent criminals, explained that the FBI studies weren't "looking at pornography. We didn't ask how often they [criminals] thought about it. We never quantified it. We didn't ask them at what age they saw it" (Nobile, 1989a).

The state of Michigan has the oldest sex-crime data base in the country, dating to the 1950s, with over 70,000 cases recorded. It too finds no causal link between sexually explicit material and sex crimes. According to Detective Sergeant David Minzey (1991), criminal profiler for the Michigan State Police, "We have gone into our data base and have never been able to pull out such a causal relationship." The American Family Association claimed in one of its fact sheets (Boycott Lil Champ, 1990) that the Michigan police found 41 percent of sex crimes to have been triggered by pornography. The statistic, Minzey explained, comes from a master's thesis by Darrell Pope (1977) at Michigan State University. "There is a strong religious strain in Pope's work," Minzey said. "Pope was trying to establish causality, but as you know, you cannot establish causality between sexually explicit materials and sex crimes. We'd make a better causality case for alcohol. . . . Our name got attached to the study about ten years ago—I don't know why. We keep getting inquiries about it. Please tell your readers that we did no such study. We're tired of getting these calls."

PARAPHILIAS AND SEXUAL MATERIAL

The claim that paraphilias are caused by pictures is unfounded. (Paraphilias are unusual sexual practices including pedophilia and sexual violence.) At the close of the Meese Commission's hearings,

Commissioner Dr. Park Dietz said, "No sprinkling of images, however deviant, can render an otherwise normal man either paraphilic or criminal. The leap from fantasy to action has much to do with character and the vicissitudes of life and little or nothing to do with the objects of desire" (Nobile, 1989a). With some flair for detail, Barry Lynn (1986) wrote in the *Harvard Civil Rights-Civil Liberties Law Review,* "While exposure to sexually explicit depictions of oral sex may increase the chances that a couple will try it, the same cannot be said for sex with chickens, coprophilia, or actual sadism. As noted by many therapists, paraphilias will not spread broadly throughout the population as a result of people looking at pictures of them" (p. 70).

The research of Dr. John Money, director of the Psychohormonal Research Unit at Johns Hopkins University School of Medicine, bears out Lynn's point. Money wrote in his 1989 book *Vandalized Lovemaps* (with Dr. Margaret Lamacz) that the derailed sexual impulses of rapists, child abusers, and exhibitionists result from childhood traumas, usually within the child's family, including incest, physical abuse or neglect, or emotional indifference. His research found no evidence that sexually explicit material causes or maintains sexual crimes or aberrations. "The fantasies of paraphilia are not socially contagious," Money wrote in the *American Journal of Psychotherapy* (1984a),

> They are not preferences borrowed from movies, books or other people. They are not voluntary choices. They cannot be controlled by will power. Punishment does not prevent them, and persecution does not eradicate them, but feeds them and strengthens them. . . . The tragedy that deprived the paraphiliac of heterosexual normality was the neglect and/or abuse of the rehearsal play and development of early life, and the paraphilic substitute that took its place (p. 175).

Malamuth, Burgess, and Prentky reported similar findings in 1991. In their studies, men convicted of sexual crimes were likely to have been victims of child sexual abuse. Burgess found that 56 percent of convicted rapists had suffered sexual abuse in childhood, and the researchers suggest that the more men were abused as children, the more they were likely to rape as adults (Goleman, 1991a).

Money reports that people who seek out specialty pornography are attracted to it because the acts depicted are already of interest to them. Those whose sexual wirings were not burned by childhood abuse will, in Money's words, never "get turned on that way"; they find depictions of unusual or violent sex acts "a curiosity, though to see more than one is uninteresting and a chore" (p. 176). Echoing Money's words, Dr. Gene Abel, Emory University School of Medicine professor of psychiatry, whose specialty is research in sexual deviance, said in 1989, "When we have done scientific studies of sex offenders, we have not found a relationship between the use of pornography and the commission of crimes, and the use of aggression. Sex offenders have specific sexual interests, and then they seek out pornography that will match that. It isn't the other way around. They don't see the pornography and then develop the deviant interest."

In his 1986 testimony to the Attorney General's Commission on Pornography, Money pointed up that producers of sexual material had been "testing the size of the paraphiliac market" for 25 years, including "the purchasing power of those interested in violent and sadistic pornography.... They are all appealing to a specialty market," Money noted, "and not to people with normal sexual imagery" (Attorney General's Commission, 1986). Dr. Richard Green, editor of *Archives of Sexual Behavior* for 20 years and author of *The "Sissy Boy Syndrome" and the Development of Homosexuality*, said in his testimony to the Attorney General's Commission (1986), "We really don't know where some really unusual sexual behaviors come from. But the evidence that they come from an immediate linking during adolescent adulthood, with what would have been a neutral stimulus, doesn't seem to hold up." Green noted that "Patterns of interest in erotic materials followed the emergence of sexual orientation."

In the years following the Meese Commission, as before it, Money's research continued to show similar findings. In 1990, he told *New York Times* reporter Jane Brody,"a person with a particular pattern of erotic arousal seeks out pornographic material that 'turns him on' because it meshes with that pattern . . . [Money] and other researchers found no evidence that pornography causes or fosters paraphilias (sexual abnormalities). . . . The majority of patients with paraphilias . . . described a strict antisexual upbringing in which sex was either never mentioned or was actively repressed or defiled" (p. C12). Money predicted that the "current repressive attitudes toward sex will breed an ever-widening epidemic of aberrant sexual behavior."

Money's findings are supported by the FBI's research on violent and unusual sexual practices. At congressional hearings and public presentations for the FBI, Agent Lanning reported throughout the 1980s that child pornography appeals only to pedophiles, that is, to men who—because of their emotional development—are aroused by sexual activity with children (Lanning, 1993). It has "absolutely nothing to do with adult pornography. If there were no pedophiles there would be no child pornography—it has no other use." Since the 1982 *Ferber* court ruling, which made illegal the production, exhibition, distribution, and sale of child pornography, it has been, according to Lanning, "driven underground and is not openly sold anywhere in the U.S." (Lanning distinguishes between child pornography and "technical child pornography," the sexually explicit depiction of someone who has not yet reached his or her eighteenth birthday but who is physically mature. This material does not look like child pornography; those who look at it do not fall under the DSMIIIR, psychiatric diagnostic category of pedophile. It is, however, illegal [Lanning, 1992, p. 25].)

The field research reprises that of the FBI: paraphiliac or violent pornography does not create criminal sex practices. The Kinsey Institute study of 1,356 men convicted of sex crimes found that these men were less responsive to and less interested in pornography than were prisoners convicted of nonsexual crimes or men in the general population (Gebhard, Gagnon, Pomeroy, & Christenson, 1965). The 1970 U.S. Commission on Obscenity and Pornography reported that violent sex criminals had been exposed to smaller amounts of sexually explicit material than had subjects in control groups. Similarly, in their study of rapists and pedophiles, Goldstein and Kant (1973) found that rapists and child molesters saw less pornography during adolescence and adulthood than did the general public. They also found that rapists were more likely to come from homes in which education about sexuality was limited and attitudes toward sex were restrictive (see also Goldstein, Kant, Judd, Rice, & Green, 1970). Fisher and Byrne found in 1978 that individuals with a history of restrictive sexual socialization had a more negative verbal and emotional response to pornography while being more affected by it in their behavior. In 1988, Condron and Nutter reported that sexual material played no role in the formation of criminal or paraphiliac patterns. Howitt and Cumberbatch came to similar findings in their literature review *Pornography: Impacts and Influences* (1990). "Indeed," they write, "evidence suggests that exposure to pornography relatively later in life than normal is more likely to be associated with sexual problems" (p. 95).

A portion of the evidence suggests that exposure to sexually explicit materials may reduce sexually deviant and coercive action. Following Denmark's liberalization of its obscenity laws in the late 1960s, "peeping" offenses and child sexual abuse declined 80 percent and 69 percent respectively, drops too large to discount as artifacts of reporting (Kutchinsky, 1970; 1976; 1985). "It is fairly certain," wrote Dr. Ferrell Christensen (1993) of the Danish data, "that both of these offenses are often substitutes, on the part of inadequate individuals, for socially acceptable sex; so it is quite possible that the new availability of erotic material simply provided a legally safe substitute." In testimony before Congress, Money (1984b) said, "Patients who request treatment in a sex offender clinic commonly disclose that pornography helps them contain their abnormal sexuality within imagination only, as a fantasy, instead of having to act it out in real life with an unconsenting, resentful partner, or by force."

The Canadian Department of Justice Report on Pornography (McKay & Dolff, 1984) also commented on the possible beneficial uses of sexually explicit material with sex offenders. "Although the specific contribution is not completely understood, there is some evidence to suggest that the controlled use of pornography can be of benefit as a therapeutic tool in the treatment of select clinical populations (e.g., incarcerated sexual offenders)" (p. 95). Some field data suggest beneficial results from a similar use of violent material. In a 1990 report, prison officials at the Palm Beach, Florida, county jail wrote that prison fights significantly decreased after the in-prison showing of popular "slasher" films. Between April and October 1986, prison officials broke up 522 fights. A month later, November 1986, the jail began showing films such as *The Texas Chainsaw Massacre 2* as part of its daily videotape screenings. The following year, between April and October 1987, prison officials broke up 240 fights—over a 50 percent decrease since the year before. Between January and July 1990, 188 fights occurred, an additional decrease of 22 percent (Cox News Service, 1990).

In 1984, Judith Reisman was given $734,371 (one and a half times the budget of the Attorney General's Commission) by the U.S. Department of Justice to investigate her claim that mainstream publications such as *Playboy*, *Penthouse,* and *Hustler* contain child pornography that converts "normal" readers into child sexual abusers. Unlike the FBI and research data, she reported that between 1954 and 1984, those three publications printed 6,004 photographs, illustrations, and cartoons depicting children; Hustler—14.1 times per issue; Playboy—8.2 times per issue; Penthouse—6.4 times per issue.

Though Reisman was hopeful of finding the key to child abuse, her results were repudiated by social science researchers including those who commissioned her study. On April 11, 1984, Gordon Raley, staff director of the Human Resources Subcommittee of the Education and Labor Committee, called the Reisman grant "an unbelievable waste of taxpayer's dollars. . . . I have never seen a grant as bad as this, nor an application as irresponsibly prepared. . . . Our examination so far further indicates Ms. Reisman's credentials as a scientist are pretty flimsy" (Howard & Lane, 1984a, 1984b). Upon receipt of Reisman's final report, Reagan appointee Alfred Regnery, who had commissioned the study, said, "Bad judgments were exercised when the grant was first made" (McCaslin, 1986). Regnery's successor, Verne Speirs, said the Department of Justice was shelving the study because "As the final report from American University acknowledges, there are multiple serious flaws in its methodology. We

believe, based on confirmation of the problems by external peer reviewers, that these flaws significantly reduce the definitiveness and
usefulness of the findings. In fact, the major objectives of the
study . . . were not accomplished" (Kurtz, 1986).

The Department of Justice refused to publish Reisman's study, as
did the American University which provided academic housing for
her work (Kurtz, 1986). External peer reviewers wrote the following
evaluations of Reisman's study: Dr. Robert Figlio (University of
Pennsylvania) wrote to American University (Figlio, 1986a), "This
manuscript cannot stand as a publishable and/or releasable product. . . . This project, the data gathered and the analyses undertaken
offer no information about the effects that pornography and media
may have on behavior. . . . The term child used in the aggregate
sense in this report is so inclusive and general as to be almost mean-
ingless. . . . From a scientific point of view, we cannot take this work
seriously to build theory or policy." To the press, Figlio said (Peterson, 1988), "I wondered what kind of mind would consider the love
scene from *Romeo and Juliet* to be child porn." In testimony before
the New Zealand Indecent Publications Tribunal, Daniel Linz was
asked to comment on Reisman's work. After listing several methodological problems including "coder bias" (Reisman used seven of her
regular employees, who are familiar with her premises, to code *Playboy*, *Penthouse,* and *Hustler* for depictions of violence and the presence
of minors), Linz concluded (Indecent Publications Tribunal, 1990),
"The report presumes a view of human information processing
which is now discredited. What humans do is organize material
within context. This report presumes that the basis of information
processing is that of a completely reactive individual who just re-
sponds to stimuli" (p. 16).

Dr. Loretta Haroian, cochair of the plenary session on Child and
Adolescent Sexuality at the 1984 World Congress of Sexology and
one of the world's experts on childhood sexuality, said of the Reisman study (Haroian, 1988), "This is not science, it's vigilantism:
paranoid, pseudoscientific hyperbole with a thinly veiled hidden
agenda. This kind of thing doesn't help children at all. . . . Her study
demonstrates gross negligence and, while she seems to have spent a

lot of time collecting data, her conclusions, based on the data, are completely unwarranted. The experts Reisman cites are, in fact, not experts at all but simply people who have chosen to adopt some misinformed, Disneyland conception of childhood that she has. These people are little more than censors hiding behind Christ and children." Dr. James Weinrich, psychobiologist, author of *Sexual Landscapes,* and winner of the Hugo Beigel Award in 1987 for the best work published in *The Journal of Sex Research*, said (1988), "Reisman utilizes some actual scientific principles . . . but then turns around and goes off into her own lunacy. . . . Reisman's statements are spooky, meticulous in their way but often unprincipled and possibly crazy."

Perhaps the firmest judgment against the claim that adult sexual material leads to child abuse came from Dr. Henry Giarretto, founder and executive director of the Child Sexual Abuse Treatment Program in Santa Clara, California, the oldest such program and a model for others around the country. "Our program," he said, "has not been designed to include collection of data on the use of pornography because the literature and our own clinical experience showed no link between the commission of child sexual abuse and sexually explicit material. While it has been clinically noted that some perpetrators read and/or view sexually explicit material, many others express their feeling that pornography is immoral. In contrast to common belief, a great number of men who turn to their children for sexual purposes are highly religious or morally rigid individuals who feel that this is 'less of a sin' than masturbation or seeking sexual liaisons in an outside affair" (Giaretto, 1991).

SEXUAL MATERIAL AND CRIME RATES

The claim that geographical areas with more sexual material experience more sexual crimes is without support. According to initial 1984 studies by Drs. Larry Baron and Murray Straus (Yale University, University of New Hampshire) and 1988 studies by Dr. Joseph Scott and Loretta Schwalm (Ohio State University), communities with higher pornography sales reported more rapes. Yet, on further research, Scott and Schwalm found higher incidences of rape in areas with strong sales of any men's magazines, including *Field and Stream* (Scott & Schwalm, 1988a). Pursuing the investigation further, Dr. Cynthia Gentry (1991) found that the correlation between rape rates and pornography sales disappeared when the number of young men living in a given area was factored into the data. There is "no evidence of a relationship between popular sex magazines and violence against women," wrote Gentry (p. 284). The only factor that predicted the rape rate in a given locale was the number of men between the ages of eighteen and thirty-four residing there. Scott (1985) and Scott and Schwalm (1988b) reported similar findings in their studies on rape rates and sexually explicit material.

In the early L. Baron and Straus research (1984, 1985, 1986) which found a correlation between sales of sexual material and rape rates, the results are far from conclusive: Utah ranks lowest on the Sexual Magazine Circulation Index but twenty-fifth in number of rapes; New Hampshire ranks ninth on this index and forty-fourth in rapes. L. Baron and Straus then introduced into their data a "hypermasculinity" rating called the Violence Approval Index and found that the relationship between pornography circulation and rape disappeared (Baron & Straus, 1984). Baron explained at the Meese Commission hearings: "The relationship [between sexual materials and rape]. . . may be due to an unspecified third variable. It is quite plausible that the findings could reflect state-to-state differences in a hypermasculated or macho culture pattern." (For an overview of the L. Baron and Straus studies see Baron & Straus, 1987; 1989.) L. Baron and Straus proposed not that pornography causes rape but that both the sale of pornography and rape occur in "hypermasculine" cultures that have long flourished in this country.

Yet research by L. Baron published in 1990 suggests that pornography is sold not only in "hypermasculine" areas. In this study, Baron shifted focus from violence against women to sexism and gender equality. He found a positive correlation between sales of sexually explicit material and high gender equality, and suggested that both flourish in politically tolerant areas. In the Baron study, the best predictor of gender inequality was the number of fundamentalist groups in a given locale.

A few researchers have studied the relation between exposure to sexual materials and insensitivity to rape in laboratory settings but unfortunately not with robust results. In a 1987 doctoral dissertation, J. B. Weaver reported that pornography desensitizes men to rape and makes them accept sexual violence (Weaver, 1987). Leading researchers dispute Weaver's findings and in a *Journal of Sex Research* (1989) review of Weaver's research, Linz dismissed the study, saying Weaver's own statistical data do not support the claim that sexually explicit material changes attitudes about rape. In their 1982 study, Dolf Zillmann and Jennings Bryant claimed a positive correlation between exposure to sexual material and insensitivity to rape, but later research has been unable to replicate their findings. Moreover, Zillmann and Bryant found no drop in sensitivity to rape with exposure to nonviolent sexual materials. Although such a drop appears in some of their work when subjects were exposed to violent sexual materials, it was not the sexual but the violent content that produced the drop. In testimony to the Ontario District Court (*Her Majesty*, 1989), Donnerstein described the Zillmann and Bryant research saying, "After viewing a sexually explicit film, 11 percent of the male subjects said they would rape. For the aggressive pornography film, 25 percent said they would rape. For the [nonsexual] aggression-only film, 50 percent said they would rape (p. 306)." Earlier, Donnerstein testified, "With sexually explicit violent depictions, the findings suggest increases in lab aggression, increases in certain—we can just call them callous attitudes about certain myths about rape. However, the caveat is you get those effects without any sexual content whatsoever. You get exactly the same effects just with the message about violence" (p. 150).

Drs. V. Padgett, J. Brislin-Slutz, and J. Neal found in a series of studies (1989) that exposure to nonviolent pornography—even if it was "degrading"—produced no decrease in men's sensitivity toward women and no increase in acceptance of the myth that women want to be raped or enjoy it. Padgett, Brislin-Slutz, and Neal employed a "power analysis," a methodology that tests what the results would be if the number of subjects were increased, and came to the same results.

Donnerstein and Linz's 1990 overview of the social science literature prepared for the government of New Zealand reported

> "no effects for exposure [to *Penthouse*-type magazines] on antisocial attitudes such as less sensitivity to rape victims or greater endorsement of attitudes facilitating violence against women. . . . Most consistently, in long-term and short-term exposure studies negative effects (e.g., lessened sensitivity toward rape victims, greater acceptance of force in sexual encounters) emerge when subjects are exposed to portrayals of overt violence against women or when sex is fused with aggression" (p. 4).

Later in their report they wrote, "Studies in which individuals have been massively exposed to this [*Penthouse*] type of material have shown either reductions in laboratory aggression or no increases in aggressive behavior. Consequently, the conclusion that nonviolent degrading materials influence sexual aggression is without support" (p. 41).

It is perhaps unfortunate that, for the many methodological problems cited in the section on sexually violent material, Donnerstein and other researchers hesitate to translate this laboratory data to life situations. This predicament sends researchers back to the field studies on violence in real-world settings for clues about the causes of rape. As cited above, these are: membership in a delinquent peer group (Ageton, 1983), child sexual and physical abuse and alcohol consumption (Becker & Stein, 1991).

INTERNATIONAL RESEARCH

Investigations in Canada, Europe, and Asia confirm the research above, finding no link between sexual materials and the commission of sex crimes. Two years before the Attorney General's Commission submitted its findings, the Canadian Department of Justice completed a report on the effects of sexually explicit material, "Working

Papers on Pornography and Prostitution, Report #13. The Impact of Pornography: An Analysis of Research and Summary of Findings" (McKay and Dolff, 1984, known as the Fraser Committee Report). It found,

> There is no systematic research evidence available which suggests a causal relationship between pornography and morality. . . . There is no systematic research which suggests that increases in specific forms of deviant behavior, reflected in crime trend statistics (e.g., rape) are causally related to pornography. . . . There is no persuasive evidence that the viewing of pornography causes harm to the average adult . . . that exposure causes the average adult to harm others . . . that exposure causes the average adult to alter established sex practices. On the contrary, the research supports the contention that exposure, although possibly producing a short term, transient alteration in patterns, has no effect in the longer term.   (pp. 93, 94)

The British Inquiry into Obscenity and Film Censorship (1979, known as the Williams Committee) also found no link between sexually explicit material and crime. Its authors wrote, "We unhesitatingly reject the suggestion that the available statistical information for England and Wales lends any support to the argument that pornography acts as a stimulus to the commission of sexual violence" (p. 80). The British Inquiry noted that in a five-year period of increasing availability and explicitness of sexual material, sexual assault declined. Following a crackdown on hard-core pornography, sex crimes increased.

Howitt and Cumberbatch, in their review of the literature for the British Home Office Research and Planning Unit (1990) reported:

> Laboratory experiments on the influence of pornography on aggression seem to be less clearcut on close inspection than most discussions in the research literature imply. This may be the result of a relative consensus amongst a small group of academics carrying out this sort of research which has attracted attention. . . . Several studies show a diminution in aggression whilst

others show increases. . . . There is no evidence from these experiments that pornography increases "deviant" sexual activities. (p. 84). . . There is evidence that pornography may be involved unproblematically in relationships without it necessarily having clearly undesirable consequences. It may be of help in overcoming inhibitions and in other ways. . . . The use of erotic material is quite common in persons who are difficult to define as deviant and in couples as part of their relationship. Few people have not been exposed to pornography at some stage in their lives but it is uncertain that the majority of those who have seen such material are adversely influenced by it. (pp. 84, 85, 95)

Like John Money and the Canadian Department of Justice, Howitt and Cumberbatch note that "controlled use of pornography may be of value in the clinical treatment of sexual problems: see Eysenck 1978; Gillan 1978; Yaffee 1982" (p. 90).

Studies by Dr. Berl Kutchinsky at the Institute of Criminal Science of the University of Copenhagen report that in European countries where restrictions on pornography have been lifted, incidence of rape over the last twenty years has declined or remained constant (Kutchinsky, 1970; 1984; 1985; 1987; 1991). In Kutchinsky's study, sex crimes against female children dropped from 30 per 100,000 to approximately 5 per 100,000 between 1965 and 1982, after Denmark liberalized its obscenity laws, making sexually explicit material more accessible to the public. In 1987, Kutchinsky wrote,

Not only is there possibly a direct causal link between pornography and the decrease in certain types of sex crimes, but also and more importantly, sex crimes in Denmark, including rape, did not increase—as advocates of censorship had expected—despite the appearance and subsequent legalization of hard-core pornography. . . . Since it was clear from the onset that most offenses involving homosexuality and prostitution have no obvious victims . . . the detailed analysis of the decrease was restricted to "regular" heterosexual sex crimes, that is, sex crimes committed by a male offender against a female (adult or child) victim. In Copenhagen . . . these crimes constituted 85 percent of all sexual offenses and had an overall drop from 96 reported cases per 100,000 population in 1966 to 25 per 100,000 in 1973. (p. 22)

Confirming Kutchinsky's data, Howitt and Cumberbatch (1990) wrote, "Kutchinksy's (1990[1]) analysis shows a growth of up to 300 per cent in non-sexual violent crime in Denmark, Sweden and West Germany from 1964 to 1984 compared with very modest changes in the rate of rape (p. 92)." In West Germany rape rates declined since bans on pornography were lifted in 1973. "I am aware," wrote Kutchinsky (1984), "that rape also decreased in Italy (where pornography is very easily available) and that most of the European countries have unchanged rape levels."

Like the European research, studies in Asia find no link between the commission of sex crimes and the availability of sexual materials, including those with violent content. Singapore, with tight controls on pornography, showed a greater increase in rape rates (28 percentage points more) between 1964 and 1974 than did Stockholm, with liberalized pornography laws. Japan, where pornography often relies on themes of bondage, violence, and rape, saw a 45 percent drop in rape rates for the same decade (Donnerstein, Linz & Penrod, 1987). In their research, Abramson and Hayashi (1984) report that Japan allows a greater amount of nudity on television and in general circulation magazines than would be acceptable in the United States. With this and the violent nature of Japanese pornography, Japan nevertheless reports a rape rate of 2.4 per 100,000 people, compared with 34.5 in the United States.

Two investigations of sexually explicit material claimed to find substantive links between pornography and crime, though without the support of international researchers. The Australian Parliament conducted hearings on sexually explicit material and concluded that nonviolent and violent sexual material yield antisocial and violent effects. Unlike the Attorney General's Commission, the Surgeon General's Workshop, the Canadian Justice Department's Commission, and the British Inquiry, the Australian Parliament employed no experts to read and evaluate the social science data. Testifying to the District Court of Ontario, Donnerstein said of the Australian report

(*Her Majesty*, 1989), "[The Australian Parliament] should have had access and, it is my understanding had access, to all papers by the same group of researchers. . . . In the Meese Commission you had members who were familiar with or who could evaluate social science data versus those who could not. Those who could, did file a minority report. The actual social science report reviewed and written by Edna Einsiedel did not support the [Meese Commission's] recommendations. . . . The Fraser [Canadian] Commission, it is my understanding, had a separate volume written by social scientists evaluating the social science research. That was not the case, it is my understanding, for the Australian Parliament" (pp. 174–175). Because of their failure to critically evaluate the social science literature, the Australian hearings have not been useful as public policy guides.

Dr. John Court received similar criticism for his analysis of rape rates in Hawaii. He identified a two-year period when sexual material was restricted there and found that rape rates decreased. The British Inquiry into Obscenity and Film Censorship read Court's work and rejected it (British Inquiry, 1979). Ferrell Christensen wrote of Court in the *Handbook of Human Sexuality* (1993), "Unfortunately, the evidence seems pretty clear that he has been grossly irresponsible if not flatly dishonest, presenting conjecture as fact and employing hopelessly weak data at best. . . . As for the Hawaiian case, it too is the figment of someone's imagination. There was indeed a drop in the rate of rape in the two years in question. But as a review of local newspaper articles for the same period reveals, there was no crackdown on pornography; in fact, there was a glut of it, and live sex acts on stage." In a 1987 article, Dr. Augustine Brannigan (University of Calgary) wrote, "John Court, a self-proclaimed Christian psychologist and one-time leader of the antipornography Festival of Light, published a series of papers to discredit Kutchinsky's Danish study. The Williams Committee in the United Kingdom scrutinized his work and characterized it as misleading and intellectually dishonest" (p. 15).

Four

I Know It When I See It—Commonsense Claims for Censorship

The Taxpayer's Revolt, "Porn Made Me Do It," Community Standards

In response to the science literature, image-blamers have proposed arguments from "common sense" that support image-banning measures. One that took hold in the last years of the Bush presidency is the "taxpayer's revolt." Leveled against the National Endowment for the Arts and federally funded family planning clinics, it holds that taxpayers should not be required to pay, through government funding agencies, for art or information they do not like. The claim against family planning clinics specifically objected to taxpayer subsidy of abortion information in discussions between physicians, counselors, and patients. The Bush administration made restrictions on abortion counseling government policy, and they became known as the abortion counseling "gag rule." Clinics in violation of the policy lost government support. Bush's regulations were upheld by the Supreme Court in *Rust v. Sullivan* (1991).

Though President Bill Clinton lifted the gag rule early in 1993, the arguments against taxpayer funding of the NEA and abortion counseling were brought together by the Justice Department under Clinton appointee Janet Reno. Using the Supreme Court's reasoning in *Rust*, the Justice Department went to court to uphold the "decency requirement" at the NEA, appealing a federal court ruling that had earlier declared the NEA "decency" requirement unconstitutional (National Campaign, 1993; Trescott, 1993; Hartigan, 1993). In *Rust*, the Supreme Court had ruled that the government may decide what information it wishes to pay for in federally funded family planning clinics. Making a parallel case, the Justice Department claimed that government may buy the expression it likes at the NEA as well. If government wants to fund only art that has passed a "decency" standard, it argued, it may.

The difficulty with the taxpayer's revolt, philosophically and practically, is that not all taxpayers agree on what art or information is worth funding. Taxpayers such as Senator Jesse Helms would not support Mr. Mapplethorpe's photographs, yet thousands of taxpayers in Ohio, Pennsylvania, Massachusetts, California, Connecticut and New York not only paid for his work through the NEA but paid for it a second time in admission fees to his exhibition. Some taxpayers believe that information encouraging abortion or enlistment in the military is poisonous and should be discouraged; others believe it is crucial to the quality of American life. The experiment of democratic pluralism proposes that one tolerate lists of books one dislikes to safeguard those one likes from the reach of well-meaning citizens like oneself who also have lists. Adlai Stevenson wrote, "The sound of tireless voices is the price we pay for the right to hear the music of our own opinions." Abraham Lincoln said more simply, "Those who deny freedom to others do not deserve it for themselves."

Another popular argument against sexually explicit material, rap, and rock is that men get ideas from them and force women to do what the photos or lyrics depict. Yet it is not sex, the positions, or costumes, but force—economic, psychological, and physical—that is women's problem. Coercion is much older than rock or pornography. The most conservative image-blamers would not refute the history that men who use force in their relations with women have done so for centuries before the camera and compact disc, and not only in sex but in every area of life. With their focus on sex, image-blamers leave the uncomfortable impression that they do not concern themselves with the wide array of nonsexual coercions. Women's intimidation begins not with the commercialized image but with confusion and powerlessness. Those who wish women well are wasting their time until they help them acquire the emotional means to know their desires and the economic means to say "no" not only to unwanted sex but to bullying and intimidation of all sorts.

Another popular support for censorship is the rapists and wife batterers who tell their court-appointed social workers that they learned their ways from pornography. Ted Bundy, on his deathbed, offered the public his conversion to this idea. It is a clever ploy; look at who gets off the hook. It is some measure of the Meese Commission's thinking that Dr. Judith Becker and Ellen Levine felt constrained to write in their dissenting report (1986), "Information from the sex-offender population must be interpreted with care because it may be self-serving" (p. 11).

Dr. Gene Abel (1989), professor of psychiatry, Emory University School of Medicine, said at the time of the Bundy execution, "What we find is that sex offenders have rationalizations and justifications for their behavior. And Ted Bundy, like most of the sadists we've dealt with, had a lot of false beliefs or rationalizations to explain his behavior. What he said, in essence, was, 'It isn't my fault, these are pornographic things that I've seen.' And we just don't see that relationship."

Dr. Emanuel Tanay, the psychiatrist who interviewed Bundy after his arrest in Florida, said, "Pornography doesn't have the power to cause the severe deformity of personality that he [Bundy] had" (Williams, 1989; Wells, 1989). Bundy's lawyer, James Coleman, said of Bundy's final interview, "It was vintage Bundy. It was Bundy the actor. He didn't know what made him kill people. No one did" (Associated Press, 1989; United Press International, 1989).

According to Norma Wagner, director of the adult sexual offender program at South Florida State Hospital, "Pornography is probably more a symptom than a cause. Just as adolescent animal torture and arson are symptoms—not causes—of a personality that is likely to commit violent crimes, sexual or otherwise" (Williams, 1989). Of the basic Bundy argument, Dr. Irwin Stotzky, professor of criminal law at the University of Miami, said, "The argument that looking at pornography will lead to violence is like saying alcohol advertisements will lead to heroin addiction" (Williams, 1989).

Dr. Dorothy Lewis, professor of psychiatry at New York University and clinical professor at Yale University Child Study Center, conducted multiple interviews with Bundy and his family after his arrest. She discovered that at age three, Bundy had begun such unusual rituals as sticking butcher knives into his bed. At the time, Bundy and his mother were living with Bundy's grandfather, who, according to family reports, beat and tortured animals, threw Bundy's aunt down a flight of stairs, and regularly terrorized family members. After repeated butcher-knife performances, the family felt that Bundy's grandfather so adversely affected the boy that he and his mother should be moved out of the house. Dr. Lewis diagnosed Bundy as suffering since 1967 from manic depressive psychosis, characterized by extreme mood changes including rage, euphoria, and depression (Nobile, 1989b).

When Bundy was arrested in 1978, he was found not with violent pornography but with magazines advertising cheerleader camps. In his early interviews, he referred to popular sexual magazines as "normal, healthy sexual stimuli," and admitted he was turned on by nonsexual fare. Only in the mid-'80s, when the court refused to declare Bundy insane and so remove the threat of capital punishment, did Bundy convert to born-again Christianity and begin collecting information attesting to the negative effects of pornography. By 1986, he was condemning popular soft-core magazines because they caused arousal for someone other than one's spouse (Nobile, 1989b).

In 1987, Bundy started quoting research by Donnerstein and Linz that he hoped would bolster his pornography-made-me-do-it claim. He failed to include the authors' conclusion (Donnerstein & Linz, 1986) that in no study "has a measure of motivation such as 'likelihood to rape' ever changed as a result of exposure to pornography. . . . There is no reason to think that exposure to violent pornography is the cause of these predispositions [to rape]" (p. 58). In his final interview, Bundy said, "The FBI's own study on serial homicide shows that the most common interest among serial killers is pornography." As cited above, the FBI makes no claim that pornography causes serial murder or other violent crime.

Barry Lynn notes in the *Harvard Civil Rights—Civil Liberties Law Review* (1986) that criminals have confessed they were inspired by "the golden calf scene in Cecil B. DeMille's *The Ten Commandments* and an Anglican church service, For some defendants, of course, pornography has become a convenient excuse for their actions, an excuse more in tune with the times than blaming 'comic books' and more plausible than blaming Twinkies [as did Dan White, the convicted murderer of San Francisco mayor George Moscone and supervisor Harvey Milk]. . . . If a piece of feminist literature led even one man to respond with violence, should it too be regulated, under a theory that it caused him to feel threatened and triggered him to act out his aggression?" (p. 88).

Lynn's question might also be asked of those who propose that men rape because they learned—from pornography or rap—that it is acceptable or that women like it. There is something amiss with the idea that men harass and rape to *please* women, or to find favor with authority figures because harassment and rape are "acceptable." To the rapist facing his victim, it has always been clear that she did not "want it." The teenagers who in 1993 yanked the bathing suits off girls at swimming pools in New York knew it was neither acceptable nor pleasurable. Men rape because it hurts and they do it to hurt women. If society wants to reduce rape, it must address the reasons why men want to inflict such pain.

Finally, one comes across the argument that nobody likes pornography and that communities have the right to rid themselves of the junk that nefarious and sleazy outsiders bring in. This is a fine argument that the marketplace briskly addresses. If material does not sell, shopkeepers will not stock it. If they reorder, someone is buying. The retrospective of Robert Mapplethorpe photographs earned the Cincinnati Contemporary Arts Center a record number of visitors and new museum members. A jury of local residents judged it fit for public exhibition. One wonders who was the community whose standards these photographs breached so severely that a museum and curator were taken to trial.

Image-blamers would have one believe that only unhealthy, troubled characters use sexual material, and certainly no women. From this they reason the women must be protected from it. The sales receipts of sexually explicit material tell a different story. Nineteen ninety-two saw $462 million in wholesale sales of adult videos and 445 million adult video rentals. The figures for 1991 were $395 million in wholesale sales and 410 million rentals. In the recession of 1989, $325 million were spent in wholesale sales and 395 million adult tapes were rented; in 1988, $390 million was spent wholesale and 398 million adult videotapes were rented (Charting the Adult Industry, 1991, 1992, 1993). A conservative estimate would suggest two viewers per rental, making 800–900 million viewings per year. In 1990 and 1991, 47 percent of adult videotapes were rented by women in couples or women alone, a trend seen even in conservative southern states. In 1990, Jack Humphrey, manager of a chain of video outlets in Florida, reported (*St. Petersberg Times,* 1991) that sales and rentals of adult tapes were up 85 percent between 1988 and 1990. "The biggest increase is in the number of women who come in," he said. "Now about 50% of our customers are women." Relying on traditional notions of female asexuality and "purity," image-blamers may be more sexist than the pornography they would ban (see FACT, 1985).

Video Insider magazine (1990) reported that *Playboy Sexy Lingerie 2* ranked sixth on national video sales lists. Rental and sales of adult tapes trailed only new releases and children's tapes in national popularity. In the Northeast and on the West Coast, adult tapes surpass children's tapes in rentals, and comprise up to 20 percent of a store's rentals. (These figures do not include adult video sales, cable TV viewing, mail order sales, adult theater attendance, or adult video viewing in private clubs.) If pornography is an $8 billion-a-year industry, as its critics say it is, surely eight perverts are not each spending $1 billion dollars per year on it. Whose community values does sexually explicit material contravene? In the last decade, when antipornography legislation has come before state governments or before the public in local referenda, it has been voted down or killed in the legislatures of Michigan, Maine, and Cambridge, Massachusetts.

In 1991, Linz et al. published their study comparing beliefs about community standards with beliefs about sexually explicit material. They found that, when asked their private views, residents of Mecklenberg County, North Carolina, did not find even those extreme materials indicted on obscenity charges to be obscene. Acceptance of the films and magazines increased after subjects viewed them. Herrman and Bordner reported similar results in 1983 and, in a subsequent study, Linz et al. (1994, in press) found much the same in the Western District of Tennessee.

Linz et al. (1991) suggested that the gap between personal opinion and notions of community standards in Mecklenberg County results from the inflated attention given obscenity trials in the popular media there. "The greater the attention given law enforcement activities by the media in a community," they write, "the more the average observer may assume that citizens of the community are intolerant. . . . This misperception, primarily gained from the mass media, may also have consequences for interpersonal interactions. . . . The erroneous belief in lack of tolerance for sexually explicit material in the community may lead people to be hesitant to speak honestly about their own opinions for fear they are deviant" (p. 107).

Linz et al. call this a "spiral of silence" (after Noelle-Neumann, 1974 and 1984). In the *Journal of Sex Research* (1989), Mosher suggested that sexually explicit material may be especially vulnerable to this silencing effect. Image-blamers may wish the public to believe that they represent most Americans in their rejection of sexually explicit material, but they may represent only themselves.

COMMUNITY VALUES

In 1990, Penn and Schoen Associates conducted a national poll regarding the sale and display of books and magazines and found,

84 percent of those polled said Americans "should have the absolute right to buy all magazines and books judged to be legal."

92 percent agreed that the "decision should be up to the individual to decide reading material."

80 percent opposed restricting access to legal periodicals.

73 percent said it was more important to protect the right to purchase books and magazines than to make sure magazines and books that some groups object to are kept off the shelves.

Over 75 percent preferred the right to purchase objectionable books and magazines over the interest of the community in removing such objectionable publications.

60 percent said restricting access to one type of magazine (e.g., men's magazines) would lead to restrictions on other material.

80 percent said it was "unhealthy" for the government to decide what they should read; 56 percent said it was "unhealthy" for organized groups to engage in protest activity.

More than two-thirds said the government should not discourage stores from selling particular books and magazines.

(continued)

COMMUNITY VALUES *(cont.)*

58 percent opposed "picketing by citizens groups to pressure stores to remove magazines."

56 percent described such picketing as censorship.

A 1990 poll by Research and Forecasts Inc. showed that 80 percent of Americans favor maintaining or increasing National Endowment for the Arts funding (Parachini, 1990; Kilian, 1990).

93 percent agreed that "even if I find a particular piece of art objectionable others have a right to view it."

81 percent said "Congress should not pass laws that interfere with our right to free expression."

Five

THE IMAGE IS THE HARM
"Objectification" and "Degradation"

In response to the social science literature and community standards data, some image-blamers make the provocative case that sexual imagery may not cause harm, it is itself harm. By objectifying and degrading women, it is problem enough. When promoted by the Christian right, this view is called "traditional values"; when put forth by the feminist right, it is a "radical critique" of gender. A careful reading suggests that the Christians may be closer to the mark. The "objectification" and "degradation" theories rely on conservative notions of female purity and the good-girl/bad-girl sexual double standard.

The idea that sexual imagery or male arousal is degrading to women is curious. To believe it, one must believe sex degrades women, that being sexual or arousing men is something good girls do not do. Only bad girls turn men on. This strange reasoning suggests that sexual activity is bad for women because it turns them into bad women. Pornography is the pictorial evidence of a woman's fall from good-girl grace. Though image-blamers may prefer it otherwise, the research data do not show that men exposed to pornography regard women with less respect (Christensen, 1993; Donnerstein, Linz, & Penrod, 1987; Leonard & Taylor, 1983). Writes Christensen,

> The 'degradation' is almost always in the eye of beholders thoroughly conditioned with our culture's venerable anti-sexualism. . . . Pornography-use evidently tends to produce attitudes toward the sexual behavior of others, including that of women, that is *more* liberal rather than less so. These facts suggest that by promoting sexual liberalism, pornography could have the very opposite effect from that claimed by the argument now under discussion. After all, it is clear that there is far less hostility toward highly sexual women in sex-positive cultures than in others. Consider the attitude toward a 'fallen woman' in middle eastern countries, for example, who may even be killed to preserve her family's 'honor' [emphasis original].

Men have long called sexual women "degraded" and "bad" because of the nature of sex. Sex insists on abandon and vulnerability. Fearing these as it is natural to do, men try to regain control even as they surrender to abandon. Control in this case includes controlling women, the sirens of vulnerability. Staying in control and on top of things means taking women down—or taking them down a peg, physically or in the mind's eye. To this end, men call sexy women "trash," "sluts," or "degraded." "For many people," wrote Dr. Martin Klein (1992), "having pornography or other kinds of publicly acknowledged sex in a community increases anxiety. . . . For them, declaring porn, sex ed, and homosexuality 'bad' helps define good and bad sexuality. This allows them to psychologically split, putting their bad sexuality out there where it can be pushed away, disowned" (p. 4). Men locate their "bad" sexuality in women and call women "bad."

Women fear the thrill of sex as well, but men have had the advantage of making a culture and ethos of their qualms. Projecting onto women their unease about abandon, they call women "trouble." The sexier women are, the more trouble, the trashier. As comforting as this may be to men, the idea that provocative women are "degraded" is neither feminism nor rape prevention but sexism.

The notion that pornography objectifies women is another curiosity. Those who promote it cannot mean that no woman was the object of male desire before commercialized pictures. Like attacks against "degradation," the campaign against "objectification" relies on the good-girl/bad-girl sexual divide. Image-blamers substitute "object" for "trash," and claim that sexy women have been turned to objects. They promise to repair the pedestal and so spare men the anxiety of arousal. Most critically, they make no distinction between being the object of misogyny and the object of desire.

As a political condition, objectification is a frightful state in which women are ridiculed as baubles, "protected" as figurines, and not paid good money. In the realms of art, games, and sex, objectification is one of life's charms. No one gets dressed up on a Saturday night to be ignored. At times, one wants to be appreciated for all one's aspects by those who know one thoroughly. At times, one wants to be desired by total strangers, to grab the attention of a room. One wants the buzz of lust.

Without the distinction between the worlds of money and power and those of art, games, and sex, image-blamers will deny women the thrill of admiration in a bogus bargain for safety. Women will deny themselves admiration in a mistaken ploy for respect. This is not only a case of babies and bathwater, it is one-stop shopping for a *chador*. Economics and politics are serious in a way that play is not, even when it absorbs one's attentions completely, as will any good drama or game of bowling. Economics and politics determine one's ability to make a living and what one can do with one's time and money. Playful activities, like games and flirtations, do not. They are designed to display the body or its skills. They are calculated to arouse admiration, emotion, and fantasy. Most important, one plays for free (Huizinga, 1950).

It is important that life be just. It is important that play be open.

One wants to meet people who treat one fairly, but one also reads of Fagins and Fausts. One wants to be the author of one's life, its subject, but one also wants to be the object of irrepressible lust. The passion of *Giselle* is play. The performers' salaries and the ticket prices are not. Pornography and fashion magazines are play, the models' fees and treatment are not. Rape fantasies are play, rape is not. Human beings are experts at noting the difference. The pretense that no one is an object in a "feminist" or Christian seduction lies to women about sex and does women and men little good. One person may be the subject one minute, the other later on, but at any moment someone is the object or the game cannot be played. It is not only fun to play the object, it is powerful, as men who want women to be good girls know.

Outside the world of play, objectification is brutal. It is there, in the realms of cash and clout, that women must fight it. Women should demand money and authority, and still play. They should also demand respect yet still play around.

Because of human ambivalence about sex, its association with abandon, it discomforts men to imagine each other in the driven, goofy postures of sex. Men have made a compromise with other men: they do not regularly imagine each other in sexual poses, but they know that every man gets into them. They do not diminish male stature. Feminism demands that men (and women) come to the same agreement with women.

At the close of the eighteenth century, men gave up their perrukes, maquillage, and brocade for the plain frock coat to assert their sobriety. They gave up theatricality and a form of sexual expression. So thoroughly were these boastful pleasures denied that it took 150 years and the counterculture of the '60s to see a renaissance, which today continues, however discreetly, in suits by Armani and scents by Aramis. Women need not make the same mistake.

Perhaps, as image-blamers argue, sexual imagery teaches men that women are sexual objects only, in life not just in play. This is a bit of theory that lives only in the minds of those who invented it. All human beings have powerful, frequent, three-dimensional experiences of women being many things, beginning with one's mother.

It is perverse to think two-dimensional pictures, sexual or otherwise, could wipe out this reality—and any rapist who says otherwise, who says he thought women were objects, is trying to get off the hook. Ambivalence about arousal and the wish to punish arousing women swirl about in the unconscious minds of most men. Rapists and batterers perform that wish in life. They hurt women, then claim the women deserved it and made them do it. They rely on the equation between sexy women and "bad" ones. Image-blamers assume the same.

Beneath image-blaming and the "objectification" argument runs a strong current of woman-blaming. Men used to get away with rape and assault with the "tight sweater" excuse. A skirt too short, a neckline too low made rape the woman's fault. Under image-blaming it is still the woman's fault, if not the woman in the sweater then the woman in the magazine. If not the woman on the street then the woman on the screen, calendar, or wall. Ferrell Christensen (1993) wrote, "Shall we say that people who drive nice cars in public are to blame for inciting car theft, or instead, that thieves are wholly responsible for their own action? . . . As everyone should be aware, attempts to cool male ardor by covering more of the female body result in enhancing the power of other parts to excite." Porn-made-me-do-it reasoning may be anchored by long tradition: first it was the devil that made them do it, now it's Miss Jones. But it is neither feminism nor rape prevention. Attorneys Nan Hunter and Sylvia Law wrote in their brief to the U.S. Court of Appeals (FACT, 1985), "Individuals who commit acts of violence must be held legally and morally accountable. The law should not displace responsibility onto imagery."

It cannot be a goal of feminism to eliminate moments during the day when a heterosexual man considers a woman, or women as a class, to be sexually desirable. Feminism seeks to expand the roles accessible to women, including the role of voyeur and sexual subject. Women need recognize the objects of their desire and partake of them without a fall from good-girl grace. That means more sexual imagery by and for women, not less for men. Dr. Leonore Tiefer recommended to women, "There is too much emphasis on sex in this culture, especially since there is no training, let alone an appreciation of talent. If you want to play Rachmaninoff, you've got to practice" (Tiefer, 1993). One of the benefits of the last twenty-five years is that men more readily admit the pleasure in being objects of desire and women more openly desire. Filmmaker Candida Royalle, author Susie Bright, the editors of *On Our Backs* magazine, and the Kensington Ladies' Erotic Society, among others, make pornography for the female audience. Starlets now properly include Alec Baldwin, Tom Cruise, Rupert Everett, and the eternally sexy Redford and Newman. (For an expanded discussion of female sexual fantasy, see Vance, 1984; Snitow, Stansell, & Thompson, 1983; & Sex Issue, 1981.)

Six

MISUSING THE
MAGDALENE
Sex Industry Workers

Most image-blaming focuses on the adverse affects sexual material is said to have on its viewers. An important case is also made against its effects on workers. The sex industries are said to exploit economically the women and men who work in them, which at times they do. As in any industry, the worse the working conditions, the worse the exploitation. Yet, it is disingenuous of concerned citizens to claim that the exploitations of a market economy are limited to the production of sexual imagery. It is self-indulgent to confuse economics with guilty feelings about sex.

The women and men in the sex industries are not stupid; they are likely making the best economic choice among those available. It is not unreasonable to choose making a sex film (at a fee of $3,000 for two days work) over working the night shift cleaning office building lavatories or slinging meat patties at McDonald's for minimum wage. Those who righteously wish to shut down the sex industries are telling performers not to eschew exploitation but to eschew it in the nude. If working in the sex industries is not the ideal job for women or men, the remedy is economic alternatives. Until they are provided, do-gooders are being sanctimonious at the expense of the actors and models who need the work. Closing the sex industries eliminates a source of income, however dismaying it seems to outsiders, and collapses options. Education and job training expands them.

Feminists who work with abused women have also pointed up the physical mistreatment of models and actors performing in sexual material. It is more than obvious to say that any one who commits violence in the production of sexual material or in any other industry should be vigorously prosecuted under laws against fraud, intimidation, assault, false imprisonment, kidnapping, battery, and rape. Yet right-wing feminists and policymakers are irresponsibly limiting a discussion of violence to the production of sexual imagery. Women are not injured there more often than elsewhere; women are most often hurt by relatives or friends. In cases of simple assault, the most frequent type of violence against women, a woman is two times more likely to be injured by relatives or friends than by strangers (Reiss & Roth, 1993, p. 232). In homicide cases, the most frequent killers of women are intimate partners; family members, partners and friends account for 60 percent of female homicides, while acquaintances account for 28.6 percent and strangers for 12.2 percent. Actress and filmmaker Candida Royalle reported that after years of performing in sexual material without incident, she was sexually assaulted in her first job as a secretary (Royalle, 1987). Sexual harassment or rape that occurs in an insurance office does not recommend the elimination of insurance. Sexual abuse in the production of pornography should not suggest obliterating sexual material. Violence ought to be targeted wherever it occurs.

The most effective guarantee of safety for sex industry workers would be provisions making the sex industries legitimate retail businesses. The more legitimate, the more accountable to law, from sanitation codes and work-for-hire contracts to criminal codes. The National Research Council's Panel on Understanding and Preventing Violence (Reiss & Roth, 1993) writes that violence in prostitution "is greater in settings over which the seller has less control over others' access. Thus 'call girl' operations are apparently less violent than open-air streetwalking, but more violent than houses of prostitution" (p. 18). All activity is more dangerous in illegal markets. A woman cannot go to the police and complain about being raped or cheated of her pay if her job is illegal or if, because the cops think she's cheap, they laugh her out of the station house. When cops laugh, they act from the same principles as the image-blamer: an overtly sexual woman is degraded; she deserves what she gets. Rather than restrict sexual images and drive their production further underground, the country might expand programs to help the police and courts respond to sex industry workers and take their charges seriously.

"Decency" advocates who focus on banning sexual images rather than on solutions to real-world abuses may be engaging in an exploitation of their own. The plight of "fallen women" is a well-known theme in pornography. Using the lives of porn models as bodice rippers, reformers may live the most transgressive adventures without risk to limb or reputation. They have their sex and sanctimoniousness too. For sex workers, this is double mistreatment. When they perform for client or camera, they at least get paid.

At their July 1991 convention, the National Organization for Women considered launching a national campaign against sexually explicit material. Performers from the sex industries attended the convention and lobbied against the idea, arguing that restrictions on pornography worsen rather than improve their lives. They have made their case at many feminist conventions through the 1980s and '90s, and yet are forced to repeat performances because some feminists cannot shake the thrall of the double standard. They cannot leave the idea that exploitation in the production of sexual material is worse than any other or that being a bad girl is woman's worst fate.

If you're a good girl, the old promise goes, nothing bad will befall you, but if you're bad, you're fallen and hell's the limit. This is the sexist's alibi and the rapist's excuse. How ironic that it has become the vision of some feminists. At a 1993 conference on feminism and censorship, Dr. Thelma McCormack (1993) of York University said "It is clear that the image of woman that was self-defeating was not the nymphomaniac of pornography but the mainstream woman who wanted to be at home, whose first loyalty was to her husband and children. . . . It is this image that sentimentalized, idealized and anything but degraded. And it is used to justify low wages, dead-end jobs, promotion, discrimination, and so forth. This woman is devalued by any number of objective indexes—but not degraded. In short, if we could get rid of all pornography, hard-core and soft-core, print and visual . . . women would still be working at 66 cents on the [male] dollar and would still be without pay equity. It is the domestic woman, not the Dionysian woman, who reinforces cultural inequality."

Image-blamers take as a first principle, as have generations of men before them, that sex degrades women. Image-blamers suggest, as did generations of gentlemen before them, that they protect women from harm by protecting them from sex. However well intentioned, these activists work from unexamined assumptions about sex—assumptions meant to soothe men's fear of abandon and the women who inspire it. The division of women into good and bad girls helps men contain their worries and their women. It helps women not at all. The double standard is a thorough reversal of feminism, which correctly calls the sex-degrades-women idea misogynist. Feminist image-blamers believe they are radical, but they have collapsed into the beliefs of their oppressors.

Seven

MINORS AND MEDIA MINOTAURS
Sexual Material, Rock, and Rap

The most persuasive case against sexual material has been its effect on minors. Protestors against pornography argue that children come across considerable sexual material in magazines, movies, and music, and that their attitudes and behavior are molded by it. Yet the Surgeon General's Workshop on Pornography (1986) found little evidence that children ages ten to seventeen see much sexually explicit material. In questioning before the Ontario District Court (*Her Majesty*, 1989), Edward Donnerstein said, "The research presented to the Surgeon General of the United States was the most complete statement of what adolescents view . . . the substantial majority of viewing really occurs in the PG-13 and R-rated form. There is very little evidence, very little evidence, in the surveys that children see anything X-rated whatsoever" (p. 167).

In their literature review on sexually explicit material, Howitt and Cumberbatch (1990) found no link to teen crime and little reason to believe that viewing sexual materials causes other harm to minors except if they are exposed to such material in the course of sexual abuse or if they are harmed in the making of sexual materials. (Sexual material portraying minors is illegal to produce, exhibit, or distribute.) Howitt and Cumberbatch conclude, "We know relatively little about the role of pornography in the psychosexual development of children except through adult recollection. It is known that exposure to such materials is common in later childhood and adolescence, but apart from reports of children used in producing pornography or exposed to pornography as part of sexual abuse, little evidence exists that pornography is harmful. Indeed, evidence suggests that exposure to pornography relatively later in life than normal is more likely to be associated with sexual problems" (p. 95). Ageton (1983) and Becker and Stein (1991) found membership in a delinquent peer group, alcohol abuse and physical abuse in the home—but not exposure to sexual material—as the significant causes of adolescent crime (see Chapter 3, "Violent Sexual Material and Aggression").

Nevertheless, many parents are concerned that harm might come to their children from sexual material. Drs. J. Peterson, K. Moore, and F. Furstenburg (1984) measured exposure to sexual material on TV at ages ten to eleven and sexual practice at age 16. They found that exposure to sexual images had no effect on later sexual practice. Four years later, Dr. Bradley Greenberg, chair of the Telecommunications Department at Michigan State University, studied the effect on high schoolers of television programs that included prostitution, sexual intercourse (married and unmarried), and homosexuality. He found (Greenberg et al., 1988) that the children's understanding of sexual terminology increased with viewing but that there were no effects on the teenagers' beliefs or values regarding monogamy, prostitution, extramarital or premarital sex, or homosexuality. Greenberg's research is consistent with studies which find that of all available sources of information about sex, children and teenagers rely most on their peers (Chilman, 1983; Mancini & Mancini, 1983).

Though one study shows that reliance on radio, television, and school sex education programs is increasing (Fabes & Strouse, 1987), a 1986 national poll found that teenagers rank the media fourth as a source of information about sex, after friends, parents, and schools (Louis Harris and Associates, 1986).

Shifting focus from sexually explicit materials to PG-13 and R-rated fare, the Surgeon General's Workshop (1986) reported that the sexual content in such movies has little impact on children at an age when they do not have the cognitive ability to comprehend it. By the time they have such cognitive ability, they are likely to be hearing information about sex from their friends. "As children mature," wrote the Surgeon General's Workshop (1986),

> they develop new cognitive and emotional skills, and their interests shift. As a result of these changes in basic understanding and orientations, the message that an 8- or 12- or 16-year-old would get from a certain pornographic movie may be quite different from that of an 18-year-old. . . . Growing up in the 80's is different than growing up in the 60's, and sociohistorical changes can affect the rates of many things from juvenile crime to views of interpersonal relationships (p. 36). . . . Speculating about the effects on children less than 12 years of age is even more of a problem. Younger children think in a qualitatively different manner from those on whom research regarding the effects of pornography are done. . . . The fear of some is that the sexual and emotional patterns to be followed by their children when they are grown will be 'imprinted' on them by seeing pornography at a younger age. Others believe that young children are less affected since they do not have the cognitive or emotional capacities needed to comprehend the messages of much pornographic material. . . . In the end, then, it is really rather difficult to say much definitively about the possible effects of exposure to pornography on children." (pp. 37–38)

As for sexual language (rather than images) in films or TV programming, Wilson, Linz, & Randall (1990) found "that children under 12 do not fully understand sexual terms and innuendoes. If children do not understand basic sexual concepts, it is also unlikely that profane language referring to these sexual activities will be fully comprehended. Without such an understanding, the negative impact of these words may be quite limited. It should be noted that lack of comprehension does not preclude a child from repeating a sexual term or using it inappropriately in a social context. However, since peers and parents are reportedly more influential than media as sources of sex information, these words are just as likely to be heard from other people as from movies" (p. 456).

In her 1989 book *Understanding Human Sexuality*, Janet Hyde wonders if the problem with children and sexual material is not overexposure but lack of information. She reports that American children between the ages of five and fifteen are "sexual illiterates" (p. 646). In their book *Children's Sexual Thinking* (1982), Ronald Goldman and Juliette Goldman reported that 0 percent of the nine-year-olds in their study knew the term *uterus*.

Some parents and community leaders suggest that rock and rap, with the engaging properties of music added to language, affect young listeners where language alone does not. Drs. Jill Rosenbaum and Lorraine Prinsky (1987a; 1987b) found that in the 600 songs most popular among teenagers, the most common theme (26 percent) was love (not violence, drugs or "satanism" as image-blamers propose). Students considered very few (7 percent) of the songs to be about sex, violence, drugs, or the devil. For this 7 percent of songs, the teenagers had a limited understanding of the lyrics' meaning, and their interpretations of the lyrics differed considerably from those of adults. Students were unable to explain 37 percent of the songs they named as their favorites. Rosenbaum and Prinsky wrote (1987b), "The major objections to current popular music point to references of sex, violence, drugs, and satanism. If youths are influenced by such themes, we would expect them to describe such topics in their favorite songs. However, these data indicate that the students hear or understand very little of the references to these topics" (p. 85). Testifying to the Ontario District Court (*Her Majesty*, 1989), Donnerstein reviewed the social science literature on effects of rock music and videos on minors. "There has been research done . . . on rock videos, rock videos which would contain violence and rock videos, for instance, that would contain sexist types of messages, and the findings are, again, absolutely nothing happens" (p. 203).

The Reverend Calvin Butts III, pastor of the Abyssinian Baptist Church in Harlem, and other leaders in the African-American community were not convinced of rap's inefficacy, especially the hardcore rap that emerged in 1992–93. Reverend Butts told *The New York Times* (Marriott, 1993), "you are constantly hearing over and over talk about mugging people, killing women, beating women, sexual behavior. When young people see this—14, 15, 16 years of age—they think this is acceptable behavior." Perhaps the grown-ups have missed the point. Young men make misogynist and violent rap because it is *un*acceptable. Rap, like rock before it, is rebellious and will thumb its middle finger at every standard of acceptability. It is an ungainly effort to make rappers and their audiences feel big. Adults control all the mainstays of life; adolescents seize the outrageous. Music and hairstyles are places to do it.

Black playwright and screenwriter Richard Wesley said of rap, "It is anti-establishment, anti-authoritarian and it is rebellious, which are all things to guarantee that it relates to youth. . . . Middle-class kids want to show that they are still down [hip], so they affect the attitude and mannerisms of kids from much poorer backgrounds" (Marriott, 1993). Twenty-five years ago, parents bemoaned the music of Dylan and Led Zeppelin; twenty-five years earlier, "Frankie" was undermining God and country; and twenty-five years before that, jazz was turning respectable girls into flappers and destroying civilization along the way.

In sum, the research suggests that sexual imagery in the media does not cause minors to commit violence; it has scant sway over their sexual beliefs and behavior. Some parents nevertheless find it objectionable and wish to keep their children from it. The great difficulty in trying to protect one's children by restricting TV or the stock of local music stores is that adults do not agree on the materials suitable for minors of different ages. One parent's literature, popular entertainment, or music is another parent's trash. Some parents believe Christian lyrics teach young people morals, and others see them as the tip of a theocratic state. Some would encourage their minor children to watch *Roseanne* and *Married . . . with Children* while others would prohibit them from reading Judy Blume or *Anne Frank: The Diary of a Young Girl*. In 1993, curricula on AIDS and homosexuality turned the normally tepid New York school board elections into a joust between Christians and lions. AIDS education syllabi were included in the new Rainbow curriculum proposed by then education chancellor Joseph Fernandez. *Daddy's Roommate* and *Heather Has Two Mommies*, novellas about children with gay parents, were recommended as supplementary reading for teachers. Some parents felt these were long overdue; others felt the novellas and AIDS information contravened their religious beliefs. One Queens school district brooked central school board authority and refused to use the curriculum. The standoff between Fernandez and local districts led to a split on the board of education and to Fernandez's dismissal.

Parents who remove material they dislike from libraries, shops, or TV have judged that material for other people's children (as well as for other adults)—a determination most Americans would rather make themselves. Dr. Beverly Lynch, past president of the American Library Association (ALA), suggests that guiding the reading and viewing of minors is the job of parents, not of local groups or government. It is the ALA's position that most parents would prefer to supervise their children's reading and viewing—not only about sex but about religion, politics, money, and most other aspects of life— rather than have this done for them by state authorities or other parents, however well meaning. Dr. Lynch testified to the Meese Commission (1986), "The American Library Association opposes restricted access to material and services for minors, and holds that it is parents—and only parents—who may restrict their children—and only their children—from access to library materials. We not only defend the right of parents to supervise and guide the reading habits of their children, but we assert that it is their responsibility." Gordon Conable, director of the Monroe County, Michigan, library system said (1991; 1993), "I don't want the government or local committees interfering with what I do or do not let my son see and I don't want them interfering with my disciplinary measures if he disobeys me."

Far from the TV set, children encounter people and ideas in life that contradict their parents' beliefs. In such circumstances, parents rely on the values they have imparted to their children to be a foundation for their children's developing views. More dangerously, parents allow their children to play out of doors in spite of the threat of traffic. They have taught their children to play safely and trust their words will prevail. Parents risk this in the face of oncoming cars. No idea, however alien or offensive, can maim as quickly. Parents have the right and the tedious responsibility to judge art, entertainment, and even trash for themselves and their families without the sanctimony of strangers. Like most hypocrisies, restrictions on media are empty flattery. They create the illusion of virtue when one is relying on the "virtue" of others.

VIOLENT MATERIAL AND MINORS

Dr. Beverly Lynch's recommendation that parents guide the reading and viewing of only their children respects differences among parents, allows them control of their children, and frees them from the meddling of other parents, but it fails to satisfy current concerns about violence. Not only parents but also makers of public policy wish to govern the viewing of other people's children in the belief that it will reduce mayhem on the street.

Nineteen-ninety-two and '93 saw a rise in concern about violent media images that in a short while grew to near panic. In 1993, both houses of Congress held hearings on the effects of violent imagery, especially the effect of television images on minors. In a public address in October of that year, Attorney General Janet Reno announced that TV networks must reduce violent programming or face government action. Though it was expected that conservative members of Congress and Christian advocacy groups would support the hearings—the American Family Association's Donald Wildmon was simultaneously lambasting ABC's *N.Y.P.D. Blue* series for violent content which, Wildmon admitted, he had not yet seen (Carter, 1993)—the 1993 sessions were notable for the support they garnered from liberals on the hill. Members of Congress usually considered progressive, notably Paul Simon (D.-Illinois), supported a labeling system for television programs. Nine bills designed to curb TV violence were introduced into Congress in 1993; pressure to take some action against violent programming rose to such a pitch in the summer months that the country's four broadcast networks (ABC, NBC, CBS, and Fox) agreed to air parental advisory warnings (a V rating) for all shows with violent content. "Many members of Congress have warned," wrote *The New York Times*, "that they would press for legislation mandating a rating system like those at movie theaters and perhaps even specific limits on the amount or timing of shows filled with violence" (Andrews, 1993a). Under the networks' plan, violent content is rated by each network and parental warnings air before broadcast and during commercial breaks. Labels are placed in all marketing and promotional materials and are available to newspapers and magazines for their TV listings.

Following the announcement of the V rating, policymakers, advocacy groups, and the press began discussing how much labeling would suffice to curb real-world violence. Few asked *if* labeling would reduce violence, so thoroughly have certain ideas taken hold in the public debate: that the country is more violent now than before, that violent images cause violent acts, and that labeling them will limit child viewing. Dr. Brian Wilcox, director of the Public Policy Office of the American Psychological Association, said in his testimony to Congress (1993), "The most recent of these studies, by Comstock and Paik (1990), examined approximately 200 of the most methodologically sound studies looking at the relationship between viewing violent programming and a range of aggressive behaviors, including criminal activity. These authors conclude, like those before them, that the effect of violent programming on subsequent aggressive behavior is something that should genuinely be of concern to us all" (p. 3).

The research Wilcox refers to falls into three categories: (1) laboratory experiments in which subjects are shown violent imagery. In the case of preschool subjects, the most well-known researchers, Bandura, Ross, and Ross (1963), showed a TV clip of a teacher hitting an inflatable Bobo doll. With older children, clips from popular movies and television programs may be used. The subjects' subsequent aggressive behavior is measured and compared with aggression in control groups; (2) field experiments in which violent movies are shown to subjects in naturalistic settings, such as boarding schools for delinquent boys, and their subsequent aggressive behavior is compared with that of control groups; (3) correlational studies in which violence rates in areas with TV are compared with violence rates in areas without TV access. The authors of much of this research, including the widely publicized 1982 report by the National Institutes of Mental Health, conclude that TV violence increases violence in life.

In response, many public interest groups and members of Congress recommend, in addition to program labeling, the V chip, an electronic device in every television set that would automatically block all programs labeled V. If an adult wished to view a program so labeled, she would have to make a special request to have the block removed. Since the V rating does not distinguish between the various contexts in which violence occurs, it would mark (and the chip would block) slasher films, *Battle of Algiers, Apocalypse Now,* and *The Accused* (a film dramatizing the horror of gang rape); documentary films about wars, terrorism, and totalitarian regimes; most of Shakespeare's histories and not a few of his dramas; and educational programming in which drug abuse, child abuse, or gang wars are realistically dramatized. In *The New York Times*, John O'Connor (1993) recommended a V rating and block for much news broadcasting, sports events, music videos and talk shows that bring to public attention such violent crimes as rape and incest.

The Motion Picture Association of America (MPAA), the American Library Association, American Booksellers Association, Freedom of Expression Network, and other arts and literary groups concerned about the broad sweep of the V label and chip have questioned their imposition, as have those concerned about the costs. Jack Valenti, president and chief executive officer of the MPAA, testified before Congress (Valenti, 1993) that the movie rating system looks at 900 hours of film each year. The MPAA estimates television airs 11,510,000 hours of programming per year. If one subtracts from this the 660,000 hours of unrated programs (news, sports, public affairs, educational, and religious programs), 10,850,000 programming hours remain. "If you subtracted," said Valenti, "80% of those hours as programs which really don't need to be rated for various reasons, there would be left over some 2,000,000 hours, over 2,000 times the number handled by the movie rating system" (pp. 2–3). That is assuming, as John O'Connor and others would not, that no news, sports, religious, or educational programming need be reviewed. If nothing else, a TV rating system would keep a few people in work.

In spite of drawbacks to a TV labeling system, the promise of reducing violence dwarfs concerns about overbreadth and cost. In its resolve to address violence, the nation will place its resources in the most effective interventions against crime. If banning the image will banish the act (or reduce it), the public has determined to ban the image. Some evidence suggests that restrictions on TV viewing are not the best use of public resources, in spite of the reading many psychologists give the research literature. Banning or blocking the image may be misguided not because it is expansive or expensive, but because it is ineffective. In 1992, 23,000 people were murdered in the United States; 24,000 in 1991 (Herbert, 1993a). Approximately 270,000 students carry guns to school each day (Herbert, 1993b). These are not figures that encourage the country to waste its time or purse.

Perhaps most disturbing to the united front of social science research is that longest of longitudinal studies, history. The first popular truism about violence, that the country is more violent now than ever before, is false. The national homicide rate peaked twice in this century, most recently between 1979 and 1981. The first and longer peak came in the early 1930s, when no one had a TV set and many Americans lacked regular access to radio and the "talkies." As for highly publicized serial murders, "they account for a small share of total violence in the United States. Despite occasional media reports to the contrary, 'serial murderers' are responsible for only about 1 or 2 percent of homicides in any year" (Reiss & Roth, 1993, p. 5). These figures are taken from the 1993 report by the Panel on the Understanding and Control of Violent Behavior and the Committee on Law and Justice established by the Commission on Behavioral and Social Sciences and Education of the National Research Council. A subdivision of the National Academy of Sciences, this panel was organized at the request of the National Institute for Justice, the National Science Foundation, and the Centers for Disease Control "to assess the understanding of violence, the implications of that understanding for preventive interventions, and the most important research and evaluation needed to improve understanding and control of violence" (Reiss & Roth, 1993, p. 1). Chaired by Albert Reiss of Yale University, the panel included David Farrington (vice chair), Cambridge University; Stanton Wheeler (chair, Committee on Law and Justice), Yale; Felton Earls, Harvard; Lucy Friedman, Victims Services Agency, New York; Jerome Kagan, Harvard; Lloyd Street, Cornell; Franklin Zimring, University of California, Berkeley; John Coffee, Columbia School of Law; John Rolph, the Rand Corporation; and Ellen Schall, National Center for Health Education, New York; among others.

"Historical data suggests that certain cities may have experienced still higher homicide rates during the nineteenth century," reports the panel (Reiss & Roth, 1993, p. 3). These statistics are supported by in-depth studies of urban life when the Gibson girl was queen. *Low Life* by Luc Sante is an excellent sketch of the routine knife fights, shoot-outs, rapes, drug and alcohol abuses, prostitution, and gang wars of picturesque New York. Any good history of American or European cities will draw similar pictures. Given that violence rates were lower in the 1950s and '60s than they were in the 1920s and '30s, one might conclude that the spread of TV ownership in the 1950s maintained low violence rates for nearly 25 years. Or one might consider that violence is triggered by factors other than violent images. Contemporary cross-cultural data suggest that one should consider it. Other industrialized countries with high rates of TV viewing, such as England, Japan, the Netherlands, Norway, Switzerland, Germany, France, Sweden, Austria, Denmark, and Canada, have homicide rates far lower than those in the United States. Such unindustrialized countries as Ecuador, Surinam, and Trinidad, where TV is new and still an elite commodity (Reiss & Roth, 1993, p. 52) have rates far higher. Women and the elderly watch more television than men and the young, and yet commit less violence (McGuire, 1986).

Investigating societies that predate one's own or that differ culturally is always a nasty business. It robs one of the importance of singularity. One discovers that one's era is not the best or worst, and one finds oneself demoted from living at a historical crux to passing along in the run-on of days. Yet, if society means to address the problem of violence, it must embrace its mediocrity and look across time and place.

The National Research Council panel reports that studies have linked TV viewing to aggression, but it lists TV viewing with other symptoms of distressed childhoods such as inappropriately fearless behavior, impulsivity, attention deficit, restlessness, low empathy, and poor school performance. Moreover, it lists only "abnormally frequent viewing of violence on television" (Reiss & Roth, 1993, p. 105), not the amounts of viewing usual to American children (no matter how high they may seem to researchers who did not grow up with the same access to the tube). In its Matrix for Organizing Risk Factors for Violent Behavior, television viewing does not make it onto the chart; neither is it mentioned in the twenty-seven detailed recommendations for reducing violence that form the final section of the National Research Council book *Understanding and Preventing Violence*. As for the learning theory that grounds much of the laboratory and field experiments on aggression, the National Research Council panel calls it an "oversimplified psychosocial explanation. . . . In short, research strongly suggests that violence arises from *interactions among* [emphasis original] individuals' psychosocial development, their neurological and hormonal differences, and social processes" (pp. 101–102).

In August 1993, the American Psychological Association came to similar conclusions in its report on violence among youth. It found that the prime causes of violence are rejection by parents, lack of supervision by parents, violence between parents, and harsh physical discipline. Dr. Leonard Eron, for many years a leading researcher of youth violence, said, "You first learn violence with the family" (Goleman, 1993).

The notion that viewing television violence is a significant cause of violence in life (and is thereby worth restricting) takes other knocks in the social science research. Patrick Cooke wrote in *The New York Times* (1993), "Since the late 1940s, there have been more than 3,000 reports on the effect on viewers of watching television. . . . Here are some of the findings of the past few decades: TV leads to hyperactivity in children; TV makes children passive. TV isolates viewers; TV comforts the lonely. TV drives families apart; TV brings families together. . . . Four years ago, the Department of Education financed the most extensive survey to date of the research on childhood development and TV. It concluded that a disturbing amount of scholarship had been slipshod or influenced by a prevailing attitude that TV is harmful."

In his review of the literature, Dr. William McGuire of Yale University is similarly skeptical. He writes (1986), "A formidable proportion of the published studies (and presumably an even higher proportion of the unpublished studies) have failed to show overall effects sizable enough even to reach the conventionally accepted .05 level of statistical significance. Some respectable studies in several of the dozen impact areas reviewed below do have impacts significant at the .05 level, but even these tend to have very small effect sizes, accounting for no more than 2 or 3% of the variance in dependent variables such as consumer purchases, voting behavior and viewer aggression" (p. 177). (Effect size is the difference in behavior between experimental and control groups. If both groups take an aggression-measurement test, their scores—or effect size—might be 2 or 20 or 200 points apart.) Examining the correlation studies on TV viewing, McGuire writes that they "usually have an effect size so small that the percentage of variance in antisocial aggression accounted for by differences in exposure to television violence is practically trivial" (p. 194). Not only are effect sizes small, so are subject populations. At times, research conclusions have been based on small effect differences in two or three people. Laboratory studies,

McGuire notes, suffer from reliance on subjects predisposed to aggression (such as delinquent teenagers), subjects who are deliberately angered by the experimenter, or subjects placed in a situation that condones violence, such as hitting a Bobo doll after a teacher has done so.

McGuire takes his findings from the same studies reviewed by the 1982 National Institutes of Mental Health report and by Comstock and Paik (1990). Turning his attention to field studies (which presumably suffer less from the problems found in laboratory studies), McGuire notes,

> The obtained relationships between exposure to television violence and viewer aggression are slighter. My own conclusion distilled from the dozen or so better studies and reviews (e.g., Belson, 1978; Chaffee et al., 1984; T. D. Cook et al., 1983; Eron, 1982; Eron & Huesmann, 1980; Freedman, 1984; Huesmann, 1982; Huesmann et al., 1984; McLeod, Atkin & Chaffee, 1972; Milavsky, Kessler, Stipp & Rubens, 1982; Parke, Berkowitz, Leyens, West & Sebastian, 1977; J. L. Singer & Singer, 1981; Wurtzel & Lometti, 1984) is that they indicate a slight positive relationship, sometimes reaching borderline .05 statistical significance but accounting for no more than a few percent of the variance in viewers' aggressiveness, surprisingly little considering that the horrendous level of violence depicted on television allows for considerable variance in the exposure levels." (p. 195)

Dr. Jonathan Freedman (1984) takes a somewhat different approach in his investigation of the research on television viewing. To begin with, he avoids lab studies because (1) "laboratory work suffers from strong experimenter demands"; (2) the programs that have been used "have been selected with a view to maximizing the effect. Moreover, the effect of one program in isolation may be quite different from the effect of a mixture of violent and nonviolent programs, which is the usual pattern of exposure in a natural setting"; (3) measures of lab aggression are but simulations of real-world violence and are "all acceptable behaviors that are allowed or even encouraged by the experimenter" (p. 228) and so cannot reliably be extrapolated to life.

Echoing Freedman's concerns, McGuire (1986) writes, "Such sponsorships and settings may result in these laboratory responses measuring obedience or compliance rather than aggression" (p. 210).

Freedman and McGuire's criticisms are repeated by Dr. Debra Steckler (1989) who notes that the instruments used to measure aggression, such as mock electric shocks, "themselves produced the aggression the experimenter was attempting to measure. . . . No alternative neutral instruments are provided" (pp. 12, 14). Perhaps the most severe criticism of laboratory studies is the body of lab research itself, which finds that any behavior will increase when subjects are "worked up," whether from watching violent films or riding exercise bicycles. If given the opportunity, subjects whose adrenaline level has been raised will be more generous, rewarding, or aggressive, whatever the experiment calls for (Her Majesty, 1989).

Turning his attention to field and correlational studies, Freedman (1984) finds that they

> have produced quite mixed and unimpressive results. A few studies found some rather weak evidence for an increase in aggressiveness following exposure to violent programs; others found no effect or even a reversed effect. The two studies with mass data reached opposite conclusions. . . . The correlational research appears to establish that there is an association between viewing television and aggressiveness. Most correlations fall between .10 and .20, with a few somewhat higher and a few lower. However, the evidence from this research for a causal relation is minimal. . . . There is no substantial evidence for a cumulative effect of television viewing, which might form the basis for an argument for causality. Correlations between viewing violence on television and aggression do not consistently increase with age, nor is there any consistent finding to demonstrate that the effect of television viewing depends on a critical period or is delayed. (p. 243; see also Freedman, 1986).

The .10 and .20 correlations are even less helpful in determining causes of violence than they appear. They indicate that the variance in violence committed—that is, the degree to which life violence increased or decreased after subjects watched TV violence—is 1 to 4 percent. Variance is determined by squaring the correlation: .10 squared is .01 or 1 percent, meaning that in a study on media and life violence where the correlation reached .10, 1 percent of the change in life violence is accounted for by TV viewing. In a study where the correlation reached .20, 4 percent (or .20 squared) of the change in life violence is accounted for by TV viewing, leaving 96 percent of any changes in life violence unexplained. As Freedman notes, rarely do studies on media violence reach correlations above .20, yet even if the correlation figure were doubled to .40, the variance would be .16, meaning that 16 percent of any change in life violence would be accounted for by TV violence and 84 percent of the violence would remain unexplained.

Other methodological problems present themselves, such as the subjective self- and peer-ratings for aggressiveness found in many field studies. The classifications of TV violence are not constant from study to study and often do not distinguish between murderous attacks, shoving, slapstick, animated cartoons, and harms from natural causes. Freedman (1984) notes a tendency to sensationalism in the press coverage of this research.

> News reports have stated that the 1982 NIMH review was based on 2,500 studies; this number gives the impression of an extremely extensive literature. The reality is more modest. The large number refers to the complete bibliography on television. References to television violence and aggression are far fewer, perhaps around 500. However . . . many of these are multiple references to the same study, to research that is relevant but does not specifically involve either television or aggression. . . . The actual literature on the relation between television violence and aggression consists of fewer than 100 independent studies, and the majority of these are laboratory experiments (p. 229).

McGuire's investigation of the literature extends beyond the studies on TV violence to studies on other aspects of the media. He reasons that if TV violence reliably triggers real-world aggression, other sorts of television messages should be similarly effective in influencing viewer behavior. Looking at TV electioneering, public service announcements, change-of-life-style campaigns, and commercial advertising, he finds paltry results. "In general," he writes (1986), "both macro- and microstrategies for evaluating the efficacy of commercial advertising in promoting sales fail to show the expected strong results" (p. 182). He found also that TV advertising failed to promote brand loyalty and that reducing advertising failed to depress sales (p. 221). Television election campaigns yield effects only "approaching statistical significance but of a very modest size" (p. 184); TV exhortations to better living influence viewers even less (p. 186). These include campaigns to increase the use of seat belts or contraception, to improve diet, to reduce smoking, or to take precautions against crime.

> Macrostudies fail to pick up effects for so many social processes, that most of us persist in our folly despite such negative results; for example, academic researchers, like this writer, must confront themselves in the mirror as educators and researchers, even while admitting that macrostudies typically fail to demonstrate the economic value of either education (Walters & Rubinson, 1983) or research (Lewis, 1982; Williams, 1973); and social researchers whose evaluation studies have failed to pick up any sizable effects of psychotherapy (Bergin & Lambert, 1978; Prioleau, Murdock & Brody, 1983; Smith, Glass & Miller, 1980) may still get up early and pay dearly to attend their weekly therapeutic 50-minute hour. (pp. 180–181)

In a seventy-year longitudinal experiment, leaders of the Soviet Union failed to persuade its citizens of the benefits of Communism, though Soviet opinion makers had at their disposal not only state television but all the mechanisms of government and culture. American baby boomers, treated to the patriotic TV of the 1950s rejected the Vietnam War, though televised actions performed by prestigious characters, like army heroes, are supposedly the ones most mimicked (Freedman, 1984, p. 243). Fed a diet of Cleaver family traditional values, those same baby boomers became, as former editor of *The New York Post* Peter Kalikow said (1991), "the most rebellious,

anti-authoritarian, dope-toking, weed-smoking, promiscuous generation the country had seen."

It is not unreasonable for researchers to suggest, as the American
Psychological Association and the National Research Council do,
that factors other than words and images prompt human action. Yet
this remains one of the nation's least popular ideas. The first congressional hearings on television violence were held in 1952, when
fewer than 25 percent of households had television sets and the violence rates were among the lowest in the century. Among youth, violence rates were on the decline. In 1945, people under 21 years of
age accounted for 21 percent of arrests; by 1948, they accounted for
15.3 percent and by 1951, 14.4 percent. In 1945, 9.1 percent of all
arrests were of people under 18 years of age; by 1951, the figure
dropped to 4.5 percent (Spring, 1992). So eager were the public and
its leaders to blame television for something that they attacked it for
problems they did not have.

Blaming new-fangled technologies for social ills is a common effort, part of the importance of singularity. The 1920s saw vigorous
protest against movies as a cause of immorality and violence among
youth. Yet the Children's Bureau of the United States Department
of Labor reported a drop in delinquency rates between 1915 and
1925. In the same period, the admission rates to reformatories
dropped from a 1910 rate of 171.7 per 100,000 youths (those under
18 years of age) to a 1923 rate of 161 per 100,000. The admission
rates to prison of offenders between 18 and 20 years of age also
dropped from 12.1 percent in 1890 to 9.4 percent in 1923. "Despite
this apparent decline in juvenile delinquency," wrote Spring (1992),
"educators persisted in warning that female emancipation, broken
homes, increased leisure time, the automobile and movies were
causing increased crime among young people" (p. 76).

Each generation feels its conditions to be unique, the inventions
of the day to alter life in a way no other gadgets have. Yet studies on
the effects of literacy have found that even that gadget does not alter
much in the way people think (their memory, the terminology one
uses, and organization of thought) (Doob, 1961; Goody, 1977; Pattison, 1982; Scribner & Cole, 1981). The relatively minor addition of

television cannot be expected to have greater influence. Horace Kallen wrote in 1930, "The fact is, that crowded slums, machine labor, subway transportation, barren lives, starved emotions, and unreasoning minds are far more dangerous to morals, property, and life than any art, science or any gospel—certainly than any motion picture" (p. 51). Yet before television and video were thought to be the sources of violence, detective magazines and comic books were irrefutably the root of juvenile delinquency (see Spring, 1992). Before comics, the nickelodeon surely gave unwashed foreigners restive ideas (see Sklar, 1976, especially pp. 122–140). In the last century, when literacy became unstoppable, opinion leaders located the font of evil in the novel (Kendrick, 1987). And in centuries before that, when literacy of the masses wasn't such a thorn, crown and church banned improper harmonics and bawdy ballads, and fig-leafed some of Western civilization's greatest art.

It is a wonder they have not banned the Bible. According to image-blaming reasoning, one should. Not only is it the most consistent set of words and images to have graced Western civilization, but violent criminals routinely report that it inspired their crimes. Charles Manson said he was roused by the Book of Revelations. The Bible has unbeatable worldwide sales and includes detailed justification of child abuse, wife battery, rape, and the daily humiliation of women. Short stories running through the text serve as models for sexual assault and the mauling of children. The entire set of books is available to children, who are encouraged or required to read it. It is printed and distributed by some of the world's most powerful organizations, which own the largest real estate holdings on the planet and which operate tax free through one of the oldest IRS loopholes.

With refreshing frankness, the Bible tells men it is their rightful place to rule women. "The head of the woman is the man," it asserts in 1 Cor. 11:3 and "Thy husband shall rule over thee" in Gen. 3:16. In Lev. 27:3–7, the Bible specifies exactly how many shekels less than men women are worth. Gen. 19:1–8 tells one of many tales about fathers setting up their daughters to be gang raped. Even more prevalent are sex-with-the-maid frolics and glamorized war stories where the fruits of victory are the local girls. In one perverse tale, a group of men ogles the blood-stained sheets of a virgin's wedding night (Deut. 22:13–21) But perhaps most gruesome is the snuff story about the guy who set his maid up to be gang raped and, after her death from the assault, cut her body into twelve pieces (Judg. 19:22–29). Unlike movies and television programs, these tales are generally taken to be true, not simulated, accounts.

Child abuse is another biblical motif. With repeated suggestions to beat children, some passages recommend it for one's personal enjoyment. "Happy shall he be," one may read in Ps. 137:9, "that taketh and dasheth the little ones against the stones." Prov. 20:30 offers this advice: "The blueness of a wound cleanseth away evil; so do stripes on the inward parts of the belly." Applying the image-blamer's science to this material, one wouldn't wonder that Bundy read the Bible long before he perused sex magazines, with greater frequency and the blessing and company of his family. One wouldn't wonder at the Brooklyn, New York, man who repeatedly stabbed his three-year-old son because the boy was "satanic and the devil's baby." According to the man's wife, Harry Ossip walked around for weeks with the Bible pressed to his chest before he went after the toddler with an eight-inch serrated blade (Arce, 1988). A year earlier, in 1987, a Fort Lauderdale evangelist had killed his two-year-old daughter by "chastening" her with a belt, confessing that he was "training" her according to biblical injunction (*Miami Herald*, 1987, January 15, 24). (For an extensive review of Bible-inspired crimes, see *Betrayal of Trust*, by Annie Gaylor; *Lead Us Not into Temptation*, by Jason Berry; and *A Secret World: Sexuality and the Search for Celibacy*, by A. W. Richard Sipe.)

The New Bethany Baptist Church Home for Boys was raided and closed in 1984 for similar "training" that included beating the children with plastic pipes and confining them to solitary, unlit cells. School administrators defended their policies by quoting Prov. 22:15, "Foolishness is bound in the heart of the child, but the rod of correction shall drive it far from him" (*The New York Times*, 1984, June 3). In June 1989, police caught the man who had methodically murdered five people eighteen years earlier and left their bodies in the ballroom of his Victorian home. John Lizt had killed his mother, wife, and three children because, according to a letter found with the corpses, they were turning away from Christianity; death before a complete loss of faith would save their souls (Saffron, 1989; Panek, 1990).

In 1987, a woman testified before a Texas grand jury about the "sexual slavery" her father inflicted during her childhood. He justified her submission, to her and to himself, by claiming he was Jesus Christ. Rebellion was punished by corporal punishment and biblical threats (*El Paso Times*, 1987, March 30, and 1988, January 14). Another woman wrote to Ann Landers in 1987 that her parents quoted from the Bible as they "flogged away at my brothers and me. I have scars on my shoulders and back, partial deafness and bumps on my head." She was eight when her grandfather began sexually abusing her; he told her it was permissible because he was like King Solomon, the wisest and holiest of men, who could have any virgin in the land. "I realized what was going on when I was about ten," she said. "I told on him but nobody believed me" (Gaylor, 1988).

The record of Bible-inspired violence becomes more dazzling when one considers the clergy, men who study religious material at least as often as others watch TV and hopefully with greater attention. Three days before Christmas 1993, the Catholic Archdiocese of Santa Fe announced that it was preparing for bankruptcy as it was unable to pay the damages awarded by courts to over 200 victims of sexual abuse at the hands of its clergy. Over a thirty-year period, these abuses ranged from unwanted kisses to eight years of oral sex and sodomy. Between forty-five and fifty priests were accused in forty-one cases; an additional twenty people have notified the church of their claims but have not yet retained lawyers. According to *The New York Times,* many of the offending priests had come to New Mexico for treatment in a church program for pedophilia. On completing the program, they stayed in the area and took positions in the Santa Fe archdiocese. The insurers of the archdiocese, including Lloyds of London and St. Paul Fire and Marine, hold that the church knew of the abuses when they occurred and covered them up, and are asking the courts to relieve them of fiscal responsibility (Margolick, 1993).

A month before the Santa Fe announcement, an independent inquiry commissioned by the Franciscan Order of the Roman Catholic church reported that eleven friars at a seminary in Santa Barbara, California molested dozens of boys over the last twenty years (Mydans, 1993). The previous summer, somewhat north of the congressional hearings on TV violence, a Roman Catholic priest confessed to a decade of sexually molesting young boys in upstate New York (Berger, 1993). A month prior, the discovery of sexual abuse by Catholic clergy had become so embarrassing that the Pope acknowledged the misbehavior and the church established new guidelines for reporting and investigating it (Steinfels, 1993). Two years before that, the Presbyterian Church had developed new policies on sexual abuses by the clergy that Rev. James Andrews, the denomination's chief administrative officer, called "a Christianity-wide plague. It is getting worse. Every person I talk to, like me, is just overwhelmed by the caseload" (Presbyterians Adopt, 1991).

Perhaps most famous is the case of Father Bruce Ritter, a Meese commissioner and former director of the Covenant House home for runaway teens. In 1990, he was accused by several boys of taking sexual advantage of them during their stay at Covenant. He resigned as head of the facility and was then investigated for fiscal improprieties by New York City authorities (Farber, 1990). Evangelist preacher Tony Leyva admitted in 1989 to sexual congress with one hundred boys throughout the American Southeast between 1969 and 1988, at times passing the boys on to church associates or his organist. Police suspect the real count may be as high as eight hundred (Smothers, 1988). Father Gauthe of Louisiana admitted to having sexually abused thirty-seven boys and one girl (authorities suspect he abused twice as many), molesting some as many as two hundred times (Associated Press, 1986, February 2; *San Jose Mercury News*, 1987, December 31; *Wisconsin State Journal*, 1987, December 13). Early in 1988, Rev. Francis Guy Haight, principal of the Baptist Christian Academy in Monroe, Wisconsin, was charged with molesting on a daily basis eleven girls at his school, including a five-year-old in the preschool program. Haight admitted that he could not "even begin to estimate how many times this occurred"

(*Wisconsin State Journal*, 1987, November 12; 1988, January 9). Philip Curcio, a Pentecostal minister in Allentown, Pennsylvania, had a history of deliberately abusing his infant son—carrying the boy by the wrists, dropping him, hitting him on the head with a wooden spoon, and punching him in the stomach. One morning, with Bible in hand, Curcio gave the baby a beating that lead to the infant's nineteen fractured ribs and eventual death (*Morning Call*, Pennsylvania, 1987, August 25).

Bible-inspired abuse may lead also to suicide. In 1979, a New Jersey boy spent a summer at a Boy Scouts' camp where he was repeatedly molested by a Franciscan brother. The boy took an overdose after writing the note, "It wasn't worth living." In some cases, the effects of sexual abuse are delayed. In 1987, a twenty-seven-year-old Florida man who had been molested by a priest when he was sixteen, hanged himself in his backyard (*San Jose Mercury News*, 1987, December 30). Once grown, victims of biblically guided violence often repeat the abuse they endured as children. As a boy, Gregory Riedle was molested by a St. Paul priest and in 1987 was charged with the sexual assault of a two-year-old girl (*Minneapolis Star Tribune*, 1987, November 28). A Detroit man abused by a church bookkeeper as a boy returned to the church and beat his former assailant to death with a religious statue because, he testified with some confusion, "he was afraid of being raped again" (*Detroit Free Press*, 1987, August 14).

THE BIBLE MADE HIM DO IT

- In the summer of 1989, Rev. Thomas Streitferdt was convicted of first-degree rape and three other counts of sexual abuse involving three women in his Harlem church. A white man, Rev. Streitferdt aggravated his assaults by calling at least one woman "nigger" (Campbell, C., 1989).

(*continued*)

THE BIBLE MADE HIM DO IT *(cont.)*

- In the Canadian province of Newfoundland, seven Catholic priests were charged with molesting boys in their congregations. Rev. James Hickey, one of the most highly regarded clergy in the community, was indicted on twenty counts of sexual assault over a seventeen-year period (Witt, 1989.)

- Ron Steckbauer, who ran a Bible study group for boys, was arrested in 1987 for what police believe may have been over one hundred incidents of molestation of fifteen boys between ages ten and fourteen. The study group was reported to be a way of finding the boys and persuading them to Steckbauer's pleasure (*Los Angeles Times*, December 10, 1987).

- Richard Galdon, a priest serving as chaplain to three Boy Scout troops, pleaded guilty in 1987 to molesting more than a dozen boys over a seventeen-year period (*Newark Star Ledger*, March 5, 1987, and October 29, 1987).

- The Southern Baptist Rev. Gary Hambright was charged with molesting ten girls and boys in the U.S. Army preschool at the Presidio base, giving chlamydia to four of the toddlers (*Wall Street Journal*, November 16, 1987).

- An eight-year-old girl with Down's syndrome was strangled in a 1987 religious "exorcism" in Jeanrette, Louisiana (*Arizona Republic*, January 11, 1987).

- Andrea Cowan, sister-in-law of Rev. Kevin Cowan of the Rock Zion Baptist Church in Baton Rouge, Louisiana, ceremoniously plucked out the eye of a sixteen-year-old boy and told police she was following this passage from Matt. 18:9: "If thine eye offend thee, pluck it out and cast it from thee." The boy was taken to the hospital days later, with his left eye dangling on his cheek, and survived. (*Baton Rouge State-Times*, November 3, 1987).

- In 1987, an East Spencer, North Carolina, minister was

charged with murdering a thirteen-year-old girl; her body, gagged and bound with wires, was found in a church parking lot (*Charlotte Observer*, August 8, 1987).

- A Baptist seminary graduate who had begun molesting a young girl was confronted by the girl's mother. He stabbed both to death (*Sacramento Bee*, November 30, 1987).

- A Hackensack, New Jersey, minister was convicted in 1986 of sexually abusing a blind woman in his care (*Newark Star Ledger*, July 15, 1986).

- Five women in 1986 sued a Chattanooga pastor for rape and battery while they were staying at a shelter for homeless women and children (Associated Press, February 1986).

- Thomas Dawkins, a Mormon Sunday school teacher, was found guilty in 1986 of torturing and raping a girl for two years beginning when she was thirteen, terrifying her into submission by cutting her, showing to her body parts he kept in jars, and threatening to dissect her (*The State*, Columbia, South Carolina, April 25, 1986, and November 8, 1986).

- Between 1984 and 1987, the press exposed eight men of the cloth who had beaten and sexually abused their wives (*Dothan Eagle*, June 28, 1986).

- In 1986, an Alabama minister was convicted of the rape and assault of his mentally retarded sixteen-year-old daughter (*Dothan Eagle*, June 28, 1986).

- Rev. John Janney Sr. pleaded guilty in 1985 to molesting three male foster children in his care. As pastor of the Calvary Bible Baptist Church in Bridgeton, New Jersey, Janney had campaigned against "humanist" literature that he felt would "corrupt the morals of youths" (*Bridgeton Evening News*, December 26, 1988).

(continued)

THE BIBLE MADE HIM DO IT *(cont.)*

- In November 1985, Rev. Antoinette Mason of Jacksonville, North Carolina, strangled a four-year-old boy in order to rid the boy "of the devil" (Gaylor, 1988, p. 68).
- Also in 1985, three Rhode Island priests admitted to the sexual assault, sodomy, and battery of several children in their parishes (*Newark Star Ledger*, August 1985).
- In 1984, a New Jersey minister was convicted of sexually assaulting two girls ages nine and thirteen (*Newark Star Ledger*, October 13, 1984).
- In 1983 a Trenton, New Jersey, pastor was indicted on charges of sexual assault, lewdness, involuntary servitude, and the beatings of women and children (*Trenton Times*, February, 1983).
- In 1982, a Kentucky pastor was convicted of sodomy and sexual abuse of boys (*Lexington Herald*, April 2, 1982).
- In 1980, Father Tamayo of Carson, California, repeatedly raped sixteen-year-old Rita Milla. He then "shared" her with five other priests and when she became pregnant in 1982, he shipped her off to the Philippines with $450 to have the baby alone (*The Los Angeles Times,* March 1987).

Perhaps most dismaying is the record of clergy who are protected by their superiors when their crimes are revealed. Carl Cannon of the *San Jose Mercury News* conducted a three-month investigation of such cover-ups and wrote in his report (1987):

Confronted with complaints that priests have molested children, some Catholic dioceses have responded by attempting to discredit those who made the allegations. Catholic officials have sought to seal court records, attacked newspapers and impugned the motives and even the sanity of those who have brought complaints against priests. . . . Keeping the details of the cases secret has been a consistent church priority, according to court records, families of victims, law enforcement officials and attorneys who have sued the church. . . . In more than 25 dioceses across the country, church officials have failed to notify authorities, transferred molesting priests to other parishes, ignored parental complaints and disregarded the potential damage to child victims.

Challenged by evidence of child abuse or rape, some dioceses have tried to buy off victims and their families. Father Gauthe's escapades in Louisiana cost the church $12 million in victim compensation. One Orlando diocese paid $3 million to the families of four victims, according to attorneys Sheldon Stevens and Charles Davis, in order to head off the investigation of five other priests accused of child abuse (Gaylor, 1988).

Men of the cloth who end up in court often receive disproportionately light sentences. According to the *National Catholic Reporter*, 130 cases of pedophilia were reported to the Vatican embassy in Washington, D.C., between 1983 and 1987. Only eighteen of the accused priests were sentenced to time in prison (Gaylor, 1988). John Lower of Tulsa molested an eight-year-old girl during a Bible study session and received three years unsupervised probation (*Tulsa World*, April 15, 1987). After a sexually abusive relationship with a teenage boy, Pastor Charles Brown of the London Baptist Church in Evergreen, Alabama, was convicted on a reduced misdemeanor charge and got a suspended sentence (*Evergreen Courant*, September 25, 1986). Rev. David Lee Taylor of the Grace Epworth United Methodist Church pleaded guilty to two counts of sodomy with a ten-year-old boy whom he was counseling through the Bartlesville, Oklahoma, Big Brother program. Taylor got a two-year prison term, a $3,600 fine and a mandate to pay $100 to the victim compensation program (*Tulsa World*, July 3, 1987, and October 15, 1987).

The abbreviated list above reflects only the personal violence inspired by the Bible, the cottage industry of abuse. Other essays have investigated the public mayhem—inquisitions, "witch" burnings, crusades, pogroms, wars, and jihads—as well as such programs as slavery, apartheid, and genocide that have been buttressed by Bible quoting. Image-blamers are obliged to explain their inattention to this record of mimicry. Criminals who cite the Bible as their guide are dismissed as mental incompetents or bluffers while the words of those who cite TV are taken as gospel. Bible banning and labeling is not yet thought to reduce violence. Image-blamers need explain why they expect better results from restricting or labeling the newly arrived television, which lacks the divine authority to convert viewers.

Those who work in the media have an interest in blaming it for life's woes. It is an homage to their sway, and TV producers do their best to persuade the public and advertisers of their power. What a coup it is to be responsible for so large a piece of American life as violence. As McGuire (1986) wrote, "Failure to find sizable effects are embarrassing both to media friends (e.g., making it hard to justify the sale of advertising time and space, the economic basis of the communication industry) and to media foes (who would then appear to be tilting with windmills). Since communication researchers tend to be in one or both camps it is not surprising that they have resisted acknowledging the small effect sizes found in media impact studies" (p. 233). However flattering image-blaming is to image-makers, the nation need not do their back-slapping for them at the expense of clear thinking about violence.

In 1993, *The Public Interest* published Brandon Centerwall's article "Television and Violent Crime." It quickly became known as a definitive overview of the research on TV violence and was saluted in image-blaming circles, perhaps because of its simplicity and brevity. Claiming proof of the harm in TV viewing, the article raises a few questions that are frequent in media and violence research, and so worth investigating. The minor ones include:

- To explain the low violence rates in the United States through the 1950s and 1960s, the author suggests that a fifteen-year waiting period is necessary before children who have seen violence on TV are old enough to perform it in life. He then cites studies that find a rise in violence within one or two years after the introduction of TV. If, as Centerwall suggests, TV violence viewed in childhood causes life violence, and aggression may increase within one or two years of viewing, the United States should have seen a rise in aggression among young people in the 1950s, which it did not. Like many image-blamers, Centerwall fails to note that the rise in violence during the 1970s may be explained not by an increase in TV viewing fifteen years earlier but by demographics. The most reliable correlate to violence is the number of men ages eighteen to thirty-four living in a given area (Gentry, 1991). The United States saw a significant rise in this demographic group during the 1970s as baby-boom males reached adolescence and young adulthood.

- Centerwall reports that the U.S. white homicide rate (white victims of white murderers) rose 93 percent between 1945 and 1974, attributing the rise to TV. He fails to note that during most of that time, from 1945 through 1967, the U.S. white homicide rate rose not at all.

- The author compares the rising white homicide rates in the United States and Canada during the 1970s with the lower rates in South Africa, and attributes the difference to South Africa's late acquisition of TV. He includes in his analysis no discussion of the political or cultural differences among the countries such as (a) the near-martial law that ruled South Africa at the time and enforced a low crime rate; (b) the recession and accompanying unemployment that hit the United States and Canada but not South Africa in the 1970s; or (c) the circle-the-wagons effect of the belief, held by white South Africans, that they were at war with blacks. He never mentions apartheid, which among other things permitted whites—especially young men, the likeliest group to commit violence—to express frustrations of all sorts by committing violence against blacks. Often without consequence to the perpetrators, such outbreaks may have provided an outlet for aggression that might otherwise have been directed at white victims.

- Centerwall reports that the white homicide rate in the United

States began to rise four years before the black homicide rate because whites were able to afford television sets four years earlier than minorities. The National Research Council data fails to show this white lead in homicide rates (Reiss & Roth, 1993, p. 51), and Centerwall has missed the larger point that black homicide rates have been many times higher than white rates for decades before blacks could afford either television or radio.

- To give weight to the small effect sizes (4 to 5 percent) in studies on TV violence, Centerwall claims that even such a small increase in a population's violence pushes the violent prone over the edge and accounts for a doubling in the U.S. homicide rate. Centerwall assumes that a 4 to 5 percent increase in aggression in the lab translates precisely into a 4 to 5 percent increase in real-world violence. It is difficult to extrapolate from lab aggression to life violence of any sort, almost impossible to establish a percent-by-percent calculation. Further, Centerwall assumes that an increase in lab aggression becomes homicide in life when the most common crimes by far—68.3 percent—are thefts. Acts of violence, the most common of which is assault, not homicide, account for only 31.7 percent of crimes. One in 257 violent crimes is murder (Reiss & Roth, 1993, pp. 58, 61). The National Research Council writes that the escalation theory of crimes—that criminals begin with theft and go on to murder—is "inaccurate" (p. 5) and that "predictions of future violent behavior from past arrests are highly inaccurate" (p. 6). In sum, when the aggression levels of even the violent prone are raised, they are many times more likely to steal another stereo than commit murder.

To sustain his argument, Centerwall imagines violence as a single trait of personality ranging "from the least aggressive (Mother Theresa) to the most aggressive (Jack the Ripper)" (p. 65). This allows him to argue that a 4 to 5 percent increase in the nation's aggression would nudge everyone up a bit and push those at the end of the continuum— high-riskers—to kill. Mark Koltko, a researcher with the Department of Applied Psychology at New York University, writes (1993), "This is almost certainly unjustifiable. He places all aggression, from shoving someone for a seat on the subway to committing a drive-by with an Uzi, on a continuum. The two acts differ in kind not just degree. Yet without a unidimensional concept of aggression, the rest of Centerwall's argument as quoted falls apart." According to the literature on TV violence, exposure to it does not affect all subjects equally. Some studies show no effects or reversed effects (a drop in aggression) on high-riskers (Feshback & Singer, 1971; Freedman, 1984; Parke et al., 1977) and on people with low self-esteem or high levels of anxiety (McGuire, 1985).

Koltko (1993) also notes that Centerwall has botched his arithmetic. Centerwall posits that 0.0064 percent of the population (3.9 standard deviations from the mean violence level) would be over the "homicide threshold" in an America without television. He submits that TV bumps an additional 8 percent of the population from below average levels of aggression to above average levels, doubling without explanation the 4 percent effect size found in studies that he cites. This 8 percent increase would in turn raise the numbers of people at the end of the spectrum, who fall above the "homicide threshold," from .0064 percent to .00742 percent (or 3.87 deviations from the mean). The United States has a population of approximately 260 million; 0.0064 percent is 16,640 people; 0.00742 percent would bring the number of people above the "homicide threshold" to 19,292 people. Kolkto writes,

> This represents an increase of just under 16 percent, not 100 percent, as Centerwall suggests it would. *Centerwall is thus grossly overstating his figures* [emphasis original]. . . . But for that matter, just where is Centerwall getting his figure for the 'homicide threshold' anyway? Who said that the 'homicide threshold' is 3.9 standard deviations from the mean? Unless I missed this somewhere in the article, it sounds like this figure was plucked from the air. . . . In sum, the approach taken by Centerwall regarding aggression is highly suspect, but even granting him his approach, his statistics are highly inaccurate and the conclusions he draws from them really quite worthless. Whether or not it is the case that television viewing would increase the homicide rate I do not

know—but I do know that Centerwall's logic proves nothing of the kind.

Throughout his article, Centerwall mixes studies that link TV violence to life violence with studies that link TV watching of any sort to violence in life. Attributing, for instance, a rise in child aggression to the introduction of TV in a certain Canadian town, the author is not mindful that Canadian TV was not often violent in 1973, the year of the study. It was rarely violent in the fifteen years preceding the study, which would allow for Centerwall's gap between child viewing and adult real-world violence. It is not clear what Centerwall thinks the culprit is: violent imagery or simply time in front of the set. If it is time in front of the set, Centerwall does not explain why labeling violent images is his preferred solution to real-world crime.

Most critically, after paeans to the mimetic capacities of youngsters who watch the tube, Centerwall neglects their prime models: their caretakers, surrounding family, and neighborhood. With all the fuss about two-dimensional imagery, he, like other image-blamers, neglects the three-dimensional ones that are by far more potent. In the millions of hours spent in psychotherapy, especially by the Woody Allen generation, one does not hear much about Ed Sullivan. One hears about mom and dad. If a child's biological parents are not present in the home, older siblings, kin, or other caretakers are. Their every gesture teaches. Absent parents also teach. Fathers who do not spend time with the mothers of their children teach contempt for women; hanging around women is not manly, except to get sex. Fathers and mothers who do not spend time with their children teach them worthlessness. Sixteen-year-old Yolanda of Watts, Los Angeles, had by the time she was fifteen two abortions and several years' experience doing drive-bys in one of L.A.'s celebrated gangs. "You join a gang for the love of a homeboy," she said, "for the love you ain't getting at home. My ma' wasn't getting up in the morning; I thought, why should I?" (Yolanda, 1993).

The National Research Council (Reiss & Roth, 1993) writes, "The correlations [between TV viewing and aggression] may reflect the joint effect of greater exposure to television violence and a heightened potential for violent behavior, both resulting from poor parental supervision. It may also be that children with a high potential for violent behavior select violent material to watch" (p. 106). Freedman's data (1984) suggest this as well. "Those individuals who prefer violent television programs also tend to be aggressive. More simply, something in their personalities or behavior patterns, some predisposition, trait, combination of environmental pressures, learning history, or whatever, causes people to like aggressive programming and also to be aggressive" (p. 244). The National Research Council concludes, "When communities are weakened by demographic and economic shifts that concentrate poverty and destabilize their institutions, conventional processes of socialization and control fail. When intergenerational relationships break down or are distorted by such developments, the likelihood that gangs will flourish and compete with one another, often with deadly consequences, is enhanced" (p. 145).

According to the Bureau of Justice Statistics, over half of juvenile prisoners and a third of criminal adults have immediate family members who have also been in jail. The more violent the criminal, the more likely the family link (Beck, Kline & Greenfeld, 1988). Among the most serious juvenile offenders, 52 percent had relatives who had also been incarcerated. For 25 percent it was a father, for 25 percent a sibling, for 13 percent another relative, and for 9 percent a mother. Thirty-five percent of adult inmates of city and county jails have immediate family who have been incarcerated, as do 37 percent of inmates in state prisons. Commenting in *The New York Times*, Harvard professor Dr. Richard Herrnstein noted that factors which predispose to violence are "transmitted both genetically and environmentally. So kids brought up in criminal families get a double exposure" (Butterfield, 1993).

These figures support the later work of Huesmann who, with Eron, is one of the leading researchers of child development and violence. A twenty-two-year longitudinal study by Huesmann, Eron, Lefkowitz and Walder (1984) found that environmental, personality, and familial characteristics (notably parental aggression and education) converge in a child's aggressive behavior—and then only in a few children in a few settings. Children who suffered the harshest parental discipline were most likely be too violent with their playmates. At age thirty, they were most likely to have criminal records and to discipline their children physically and severely, supporting the idea that violence in the home is the definitive teacher. Huesmann, Eron and Yarmel (1987) found also that aggression in youth leads to loss of friends—which in turn fosters more aggression—and to poor intellectual performance. Children who do poorly in school or who cannot keep up with their friends feel frustrated, stigmatized as "dumb," and are more likely to act aggressively. In its report on American literacy (Adult Literacy in America, 1993), the Department of Education found that half of the nation's 191 million adults could not calculate the length of a bus trip from a schedule or write a letter about a billing error. Ten percent have difficulty reading and writing, and figures for functional illiteracy were higher. Tested for reading comprehension, arithmetic, and the ability to fill out documents, 40 to 44 million Americans could not sum figures on a sales receipt, determine the difference in price between two items, find an intersection on a street map, or fill out a simple form that asks for basic autobiographical information. Forty million people who scored at the next highest level nevertheless could not answer questions about a newspaper article they were asked to read, or write a paragraph summarizing information on a chart. Sixty-one million Americans ranked at the next highest or middle level, 11 million one level higher, and close to 40 million at the highest level. "We have estimated," said Brenda Bell, vice president for marketing for the National Alliance of Business, which works in adult training and education, "that only about 25 percent of the adult population is highly literate" (Celis, 1993). Adults earning higher incomes performed better than those with lower incomes; white adults performed better than Hispanics and Asians, largely because many Hispanics and Asians were born outside the United States. (the test was given in English). The Department of Education reported that black Americans scored poorly because they were more likely to have attended public schools where education was below standard.

To founder at summing a sales receipt or reading a map is a humiliating experience in literate, technologically advanced societies. Perhaps the high violence rates in the U.S.—as compared with other industrialized nations—is linked to an education system that fails so many students. It may not be television viewing that sets U.S. violence rates closer to Ecuador's than to France's but poor schooling. At least it is an idea worth testing.

Singer, Singer, and Rapaczynski (1984) report that child aggression correlates with restlessness, physical discipline by parents, and heavy TV viewing (not of violent programming). The authors ponder the relationship between the last two factors, parent aggression and unusually high amounts of TV viewing by children. It is possible that parent rages and neglect prompt TV viewing as well as teach children violence. Time in front of the tellie may not cause life violence; abuse by parents may cause both. In the summer of 1993, the House of Representatives cut $131 million from federal antidrug programs in schools and $100 million for treatment of drug and alcohol addiction (Herbert, 1993c). It cut the budget for youth apprenticeship programs by three-quarters, granting $34 million rather than the original $135 million. It cut aid to schools serving underprivileged children from $200 million to nothing (The Budget Fight Has Just Begun, 1993). Perhaps the public need ask if sounder policy would fund these programs rather than hearings about flickering tubes.

Eight

THE "UNMENTIONABLE OBVIOUS"

Recommendations for Reducing Sexual and Nonsexual Violence

PUBLIC POLICY RECOMMENDATIONS

In his review of the literature on TV and real-world violence, William McGuire (1986) wrote, "Research on the issue has failed to transmit a clear signal to policymakers (Roland, 1983) perhaps—as Gertrude Stein said of her city of origin—because there is no 'there' there" (p. 197). Finding such a "clear signal"—that is, finding that violent images cause real-world violence—is not a matter of discovering that images interact with their audiences. They do; but images direct neither thought nor action. If they did, every reigning culture would have a permanent hold on its residents. No invention, heresy, or change in fashion would be possible. Luther's mind would have been frozen by the Pope, Jefferson's by George III, and Darwin and

Freud's by Luther. The blacks who read "WHITES ONLY" more consistently than any child watches TV would not have forged the Civil Rights movement. Girls who watched *Father Knows Best* could not have built feminism, and all the good books of civilization would have by now created a just world. They have not because the mind is a wayward thing.

As each word or image drops into consciousness, it slogs around with all the other words and images there and, most critically, with all real-world experiences in memory. One comes to conclusions from what's left at the end of the day when the mental boxing is over. And the sparring begins again when one dreams. Experience is the strongest boxer and leaves the deepest marks. To intervene in real-world violence, one must intervene in the real world. This is the "unmentionable obvious," to borrow Gore Vidal's phrase from *United States: Essays 1952–1992*. The danger of image restriction is that, though it will limit something that interacts with the mind, it may address neither the necessary nor sufficient conditions for violence.

Crime rates in the United States began to rise in the 1970s. Image-blamers posit that early childhood viewing triggers later violence. Yet the TV of the 1950s, when the young adults of the 1970s were at the crucial viewing age, was rarely violent, and even less so at hours when children were awake. In his review of the field literature, Freedman (1984) found that "on serious acts of violence, the relation with nonviolent viewing is stronger than with violent viewing" (p. 238). If violent images do not teach life violence, perhaps frequent TV viewing correlates positively with aggression because kids over-watch TV in places where the roots of aggression flourish: neglectful or abusive homes. Where there is fighting, intimidation, or contempt among family members, children learn these are the way of the world and often mimic them. They are also likely to escape to the streets, where they may befriend drugs or gangs—that is, other kids who need to get out of the house. Younger children may escape into TV, which has the advantage over books of a volume button that can be turned up to drown out screaming and smother loss. This is also an advantage of rock and rap.

Thomas French has been a reporter and researcher on schools

since the early 1980s. He wrote (1993), "Sitting in class, listening to kids share their secret stories of their lives, you begin to understand why so many contemplate suicide, drop out, become pregnant, turn to alcohol and other drugs, numb themselves with hours of mindless TV and give up on any notion of the future." The 1993 Metropolitan Life Survey of the American Teacher found the majority of teachers believe increasing parental attention to their children's schooling should be the first priority of the nation's education policy. Forty percent of teachers who consider leaving the profession cite neglectful or uncooperative parents as a major factor (French, 1993). Walter Anderson, author of *Read with Me*, wrote about parents and schooling, "Whatever our feelings about the structure of American families, a simple truth prevails: A child who is read to at home is better prepared for school than a child who is not. Children whose parents read to them have better vocabularies, can better understand teachers' instructions, are better prepared to function academically" (Anderson, 1993).

Sonia Nieto, one of the leading researchers in contemporary education, wrote in *Affirming Diversity* (Nieto, 1992),

> the research is quite clear on the effectiveness of parent and community involvement: In programs with a strong component of parent involvement students are consistently better achievers than in otherwise identical programs with less parent involvement. In addition, students in schools that maintain frequent contact with their communities outperform those in other schools. These positive effects persist well beyond the short term. For example, children of color and from low-income families who participated in preschool programs with high levels of parent involvement were still outperforming their peers when they reached senior high school. (p. 81).

Given the link between neglect by parents, poor intellectual performance in children, and later aggression and poverty, these statements do not bode well for a country that focuses on TV labeling as a remedy to violence. (For a fuller discussion of the effect of parental involvement on student school success see, Henderson, 1987; and

Stevenson & Baker, 1987.) Dr. Patti Britton is a consultant to the State of Arizona Department of Education on its health education curriculum and has worked for twenty-two years in the area of human sexuality and HIV/AIDS prevention. She said of children and violence, "Abuse causes abuse" (Britton, 1993b).

In August 1993, the American Psychological Association (APA) reported, in its study on children and violence, that abuse, rejection, and neglect by parents are the central causes of violence in children. The APA cites other factors as well, including poverty and the belief that educational and job opportunites are closed because of racial or ethnic discrimination; the failure to learn nonaggressive ways to deal with frustration (parents who handle their frustrations with violence aggravate the predicament); poor performance in school, which makes children feel stigmatized and unliked; and failure to learn the social cues that allow children to interact agreeably with their peers. The APA recommended most highly school programs that teach children such social and emotional skills as managing anger, negotiating, and solving disagreements in ways that do not involve intimidation or violence. It suggested also that the law should require gun purchasers to be of voting age, go through a background check, and pass a test on gun safety.

The National Research Council's Panel on Understanding and Preventing Violence (Reiss & Roth, 1993) arranges the factors that predispose to violent behavior into three groups. Biological factors include genetic and physiological traits (neurochemical, neuroendocrine) and the chronic use of psychoactive substances. Individual factors include temperament, cognitive ability, learned social responses, social/communication skills, and self-identification in a social hierarchy. Social factors include concentrations of poverty, large income inequality between rich and poor, population turnover, family disruption, oppositional cultures, sex role socialization, illegal markets, gangs, and opportunities for violence (p. 20). "For illegal psychoactive drugs," the panel continues, "the illegal market itself accounts for far more violence than pharmacological effects" (p. 14, see also p. 16). Since success in illegal markets requires violence, the more markets, the more mayhem. The predicament worsens as criminals gain prestige, ousting other community leaders, and as costly showpieces of success trigger thefts and quarrels which cannot be resolved through legal means. As they too are solved by violence, the neighborhood loses faith in the policing abilities of authorities, and neighbors buy guns to protect themselves.

The National Research Council panel finds that greater availability of guns is not linked to higher amounts of violence. However, as gun injuries leave graver consequences, "making guns less available in high-risk situations (e.g., in the hands of unsupervised juveniles and others barred from legal gun markets, in homes with histories of family violence, in 'fighting bars') might reduce the number of homicides" (p. 18). The National Research Council's main recommendations to reduce violence involve long-term investigations into the causes of crime; these need be linked to community projects that reduce the activities of gangs and illegal markets and that treat substance abuse and domestic violence (pp. 21–27). The authors of the report stress in-depth, multiple approaches to groups and individuals, the best ones being "global, using multiple social learning and behavioral interventions simultaneously" (p. 107). Simpler solutions have shown effects only in the laboratory and for the short term.

These proposals do not suggest good results from media labeling, which has not yet been called in-depth or well rounded. Even studies on social "remedies" more extensive than labeling found only short-lived lab results. The efforts by Eron (1986) and Eron & Huesmann (1984) to reduce violence by showing children prosocial TV programs were disappointing. Recommendations to reduce sexual violence also do not point to labeling as an effective tool. The Surgeon General's Workshop (1986) recommended instead a media literacy program, not unlike that suggested by the National Research Council and the APA regarding nonsexual violence. The Surgeon General's Workshop wrote, "Several studies (Check & Malamuth, 1984; Malamuth & Check, 1984; Krafka, 1985; Donnerstein, 1986) have shown that presentations outlining the ways that violent sexual material can foster or reinforce incorrect beliefs or negative attitudes have been able to prevent the expected results of exposure. In other words, educating people about the possible effects of exposure, in conjunction with exposure, appears to reduce or eliminate the shifts in attitudes that are usually seen after exposure" (p. 50).

Dr. Margaret Intons-Peterson, professor of psychology at Indiana University and former editor of the *Journal of Experimental Psychology*, came to similar results in 1987. She found that exposure to sexually explicit or violent films had no effect on attitudes about rape and did not increase lab aggression toward women if subjects were given general information about male–female relationships or rape. She and Dr. Roskos-Ewoldsen came to these findings again in 1989, as did Donnerstein in work throughout the 1980s. Donnerstein told the District Court of Ontario (*Her Majesty*, 1989),

> We have also done it by having subjects videotape themselves, write essays about rape and about the problems of mass media violence . . . and you also get decreases. This, in conjunction with a vast amount of research with children and adolescents on intervention programs—the word is sometimes called critical viewing skills—suggests very strongly to the scientific community, as it did to our Surgeon General, that these types of programs would be and could be incredibly effective as an intervention against exposure to all types of media. . . . If we could construct educational programs, prebriefing interventions, then it is my firm belief that we in fact could mitigate the negative impact of this type of material. . . . You don't do it right before the person sees it in the theater. You go ahead and make these educational programs for adolescents and children so that when they do in fact confront the material, they see it differently. (p. 210)

Two years later, Linz, Wilson, and Donnerstein (1992) considered the effectiveness of three approaches to media violence: government restrictions on media; voluntary film and TV labeling by the entertainment industries; and media education. They concluded, "The solution we find most promising is educational interventions specifically directed to changing beliefs about rape and sexual violence" (p. 167).

The U.S. Commission on Civil Rights (1974; 1979; 1981) and the National Advisory Council on Economic Opportunity (1981) took a different approach to reducing sexual violence. It too did not point to labeling. The commissions suggested that public policy address the economic, community, and family structures that prompt violence against women, such as educational and economic discrimination, including a sex-segregated labor market and devaluation of traditional "women's work" (see also Boylan & Taub, 1981; *Bruno v, McGuire*, 1978; Schechter, 1982). Female poverty teaches men to consider women burdens, stiflers, and drags on their freedom. Women in turn often do not have the economic means and access to day care that would enable them to leave abusive settings. In their work on welfare reform, Dr. Mimi Abramovitz, professor of sociology at Hunter College, and Frances Fox Piven, author of *Regulating the Poor*, wrote about male distaste for female "dependency." "[I]t's all right for people to receive money from Social Security or defense contracts or bank bailouts. Only Government largess to poor mothers ruins character, breaks up families, weakens the economy, and bloats the budget. To listen to the male critics, you would think the welfare rolls were mushrooming and spending was spiraling out of sight." Aid to Families with Dependent Children, they note, is 1 percent of the federal budget, and welfare rolls stabilized in the early 1970s at 3.6 million families, increasing only with the recession of 1989 (Abramovitz & Piven, 1993).

America's impatience with "dependent" women is in part economic, in part emotional. Like most anger at women, it is fueled by the experiences of sex and childhood. The biological aspects of sex cannot be changed; child-rearing likely can be.

FANTASIES AND FORBIDDEN MIRRORS: THE IMAGE-BLAMER'S QUIXOTIC JOUST

Human beings are wired for reasons of survival to be alert and in control; loss of control is titillating and frightening. Such is the excitement of roller coasters, monster movies (Kendrick, 1991; Twitchell, 1985), alcohol, and sex. Much as human beings want sex, they also fear it and are angry at triggers to sexual vulnerability. Subliminally if not consciously, a component of male heterosexuality is a fear of arousal and anger at the women who inspire it. The mechanics of male sexuality worsen matters, with erections that are out of conscious control and ejaculations that are a loss of self. The fear and anger inherent in sex show up in dreams, fantasies, and cultural product, which are the proper places for them.

Anger at women stems also from domestic arrangements that leave mom as the prime, often only, caretaker of small children. Even in progressive households, women continue to do most of the child care. To the infant and small child, mom is the font of affection, food, and warmth. It is on mom that all one's infantile expectations for care are foisted, and all one's earliest disappointments blamed. An infant gets wet, cold, or hungry; it learns to expect mom. When its needs are not immediately met, it gets angry at mom (Chodorow, 1978; Dinnerstein, 1976). This dependence is untenable to the adult mind, though one would like the attentions of childhood. Through the rest of one's life, one wrestles with the dilemma of how to be coddled without smothering. As the infant grows, mobility and dexterity, being out of diapers and in clothes constitute autonomy and the ability to survive on his or her own. Being naked, restrained, or out of control calls up memories of infancy, alluring and threatening. Sex, with its inherent abandon, stirs these memories inevitably if unconsciously. The passion for letting go—for being like infants again—and the fear of it are at the heart of human sexuality. One turns oneself on with the temptation and the terror.

This does not serve women well, as mom is implicated at every turn(on). Whatever fears of dependence one needs to get over while growing up, one needs to get over her. She is the star of every childhood disappointment and memory of helplessness, yet she embodies the best care and pleasure one has received. One is ever wanting her and then wanting to let her have it. By the time dad comes into focus, the child has considerably more control of the world, with some mobility and dexterity, perhaps speech. Dad's authority will never carry the menace of mom's earlier omnipotence. He may be a way out of her domain. Under traditional child-rearing schemes, boys identify with dad and girls attach themselves to him in order to escape mom's morass. Later, they act out their desire for mom's attention and their rage that she's not always there on all the women in the rest of their lives. Like the fears spawned by the biological properties of sex, this too shows up in private and public fantasies, in music, movies, novels, and plastic arts, in advertising and fashion. It shows up as well in sexual fantasies and in the ambivalence women feel for other women. In a roundtable discussion organized by *The Village Voice* (Rosier, 1993), one woman said, "I dated someone who slept with a friend of mine, and I was disappointed in him, but I wasn't as angry as I was at my friend, whom I trusted. And I think that's one reason why I know I judge women more, because I expect more of them" (p. 33). Expectations for mom's perfect attention fuel male and female criticisms of women. This is called sexism and impedes women. A better place for anger at women is in one's fantasies, where one may act out in private. Ironically, pornography may not be the worst expression of anger at women but the best place for it.

Fantasy—from dreams to gothic horror to pornography—is the irreal arena where one enacts precisely what one does not do in life. For many people, one childhood mastery—dressing oneself, walking—becomes the synedoche for all autonomy and the symbol of self. Loss of this specific control is then especially arousing. Clothes may signal control and integrity while nakedness suggests the ultimate thrill and final dissolution. Mobility may mean command and cohesion while restraint calls up the threat of annihilation. Whatever one's specialty, it will appear in the fantasies one dreams and buys. These let one grapple with old anxieties and work them out, till the next time. As with roller coasters and horror films, one alarms oneself with the possibility of extinction and yet emerges intact, as planned.

Human beings tinker with fear in dreams and sexual fantasies to assuage its threat, to live with self-confidence and self-respect the rest of the time. This irreal theater is in part the "return of the repressed"; it has been explored by thinkers on the subject since Freud coined the phrase, including authors as varied as Robert Stoller, Susan Sontag, J. Huizinga, Bruno Bettelheim, and John Money, among many others. Dr. Arnold Cooper of Cornell University wrote, "The underlying emotional issues are from what the child experiences as cruelties, ranging from physical abuse to an uncaring parent to the sometimes terrifying passivity an infant can feel" (Goleman, 1991b). Siegfried Kracauer (1960) explained the workings of fantasy through the myth of Perseus and Medusa. Looking at Medusa's head turned men to stone, and so Athena told Perseus never to gaze directly upon Medusa but only at her reflection in his shield. "Now of all the existing media," wrote Kracauer, "the cinema alone holds up a mirror to nature. Hence our dependence on it for the reflection of happenings which would petrify us were we to encounter them in real life. The film screen is Athena's polished shield" (p. 305).

Fantasy has the flimsiest obligations to reality. It has no obligations to equality and liberty or any other principle by which one organizes a good society. It is a theater for what is inappropriate under the scrutiny of day and justice. Schematic, hermetic, ritualistic, and exaggerated, fantasies are playgrounds for desires so fierce one does not want them and fears so awful one cannot face them—except in the words and images of dreams, art, and entertainment. They offer the most extreme set pieces: one has sex with a man or woman whom one thinks one could never in life attract; one unlocks fear of loss and abandonment; one hits a homer, wins an Oscar, conquers space or cancer; one confronts the Blob, Boss, Death, Daddy, or the Bad Mommy in all her wicked-witch guises, and wins. In *Last Action Hero*, directed by John McTiernan, a young boy is held up at knife point by a drug addict who has broken into the family's apartment and who chains the boy to the bathroom fixtures. It is no mystery to filmgoers why that boy likes the action movies of Jack Slater (played by Arnold Schwarzenegger), where the bad guys are breezily blown to bits. Youngsters who regularly see contempt, intimidation, hitting, or shooting know these things hurt. Fantasy is where they survive them, which is not a surety in life. It is where one may encounter everything, and emerge the victor, oneself, in the safety of one's seat.

Male desire for, fear of, and anger at women is the stuff of male sexual fantasy. It is where men plunge into the abandon inherent in sex, best it, and survive. Penetrating the *vagina dentata*, they prevail (see Lynne Segal, *Slow Motion: Changing Masculinities Changing Men,* 1990). Just as sexual imagery did not invent desire for or rage at women, banning or restricting such imagery will not end them. The idea that what happens in fantasy happens in life is neither science nor feminism but voodoo. (Pally, 1985b; Teller, 1992). A forbidden mirror to life, enlarging fear and desire as it reflects, fantasy is a linchpin of sanity. No person or society has lived without it. With it, one brokers what one cannot in the workaday world. Bisons on cave walls and sex videos have this in common. Image-blamers, with their naive learning theory, misunderstand fantasy. Taking imagery as a recipe, they oppose it because they fear its mimicry. Audiences, they believe, will see sex, interracial sex, homosex, sadomasochistic or violent sex and commit it in droves. In the winter of 1992, a school district in Jacksonville, Florida, put *Snow White and the Seven Dwarfs* on their restricted book list. One must conclude that the works of Bruno Bettelheim had been restricted there for some time (Associated Press, 1992).

To reduce violence in life, one must look at the life experiences that teach where and how to deploy aggression. Fear and anger may always be a component of sex; men may forever be a bit angry at women. How will they act on it? Real-world violence is learned in the nonfantasy, three-dimensional pedagogy of family and community. In every nuance and gesture, one generation instructs the next in the sorts of contempt and violence that are acceptable and expected. The National Research Council (Reiss & Roth, 1993) wrote, "Four commonly suggested causes of family violence are chronic alcohol use, social isolation of the family, depression, and some intergenerational mechanism through which a high potential for violent behavior is transmitted from parents to children" (pp. 10–11; see also Eron & Huesmann, 1987; 1990).

To stop the heritage of violence, four areas need addressing:

1. Boy training that makes bullying and violence not only an acceptable response to fear and frustration but a manly one—

not only accepted but expected—and that teaches boys that the thrill of dominance is their due. In *Men, Women and Aggression* (1993) Anne Campbell writes, "Both sexes see an intimate connection between aggression and control, but for women aggression is the *failure* of self-control, while for men it is the imposing of control over others. Women's aggression emerges from their inability to check the disruptive and frightening forces of their own anger. For men, it is a legitimate means of assuming authority over the disruptive and frightening forces in the world around them;"

2. Girl training that teaches girls nervous, ingratiating self-presentations and an overreliance on pleasing others at the expense of self-respect and authority. These make women dismissible, easy targets for contempt and violence. When a woman thinks she must be nice at all costs, it will cost her a great deal;

3. Mom-only (or mostly) child care traditions that prevent men from taking a role equal to that of women in the care of children;

4. The patterns of sexism taught daily in the home: not only a man slapping his wife around but also one who walks away while she is talking or spits out, "Aw, shut up."

"Pornography is not the ultimate citadel of sexism," wrote Dr. William Simon (1987), professor of sociology at the University of Houston and author of *The Post-Modernization of Sex*. "At best, it is a shadow cast by more important, more affluent, and far more powerful institutions" (p. 28). As if echoing Simon, Dr. Larry Baron wrote the same year, "The [Meese] commission would have us believe that sexual aggression can be controlled through the strict regulation of obscene materials, an illusion that shifts our attention away from the structural sources of rape. . . . such as issues as sexism, racism, poverty and a host of other factors ignored in the [Meese Commission] *Final Report*" (p. 12).

To address violence, one might do better not to ban Madonna but to ban mom from the home half the time, and get dad back in.

Drs. Simon and Baron expose the irony of the last decade. The Reagan and Bush administrations were most active in restricting sexual material in the name of benefiting women and children while they cut funding from Women, Infant and Children nutrition programs, from pre- and postnatal care, day care, and child health and education services. The fundamentalists who work tirelessly to ban books, music and TV in the name of protecting women would return them, according to religious doctrine, to the economic and social dependence from which women have begun to escape. Right-wing feminists would enshrine women on the purity pedestal women have struggled to fell.

In view of violence's excellent record for centuries before the printing press and camera, the restriction of words and images seems to have only disadvantages. Were this country to ban "bad" images tomorrow, it would be left with violence and sexual and drug abuses while establishing dangerous precedents for stifling such works as *Anne Frank: The Diary of a Young Girl,* the *Maja Desnuda,* AIDS education, and Maya Angelou's *I Know Why the Caged Bird Sings.* Women should be keen to the value of free expression. With its protection of ideas that many citizens believe are dangerous, it has safeguarded the feminist social critique (FACT, 1985; Feminists for Free Expression, 1992a). Twenty-five years ago, many Americans thought feminism anarchic. Today, should women abandon free speech rights for a quick fix to sexism and violence, feminist works would be the first to feel the "fix." It has been another irony of the decade that sexual material made by and for women has felt the brunt of attacks and regulations proposed by right-wing feminists. The video exhibit by feminist women that was dismantled by other feminist women at the University of Michigan Law School has been described in the opening chapter of this volume. In 1991, Catharine MacKinnon worked with the Canadian courts to change their obscenity laws and succeeded in establishing new legal standards.

Writing an *amicus* brief in the case of *Butler v. Her Majesty the Queen*, MacKinnon persuaded the government to outlaw material that is, among other things, "degrading" to women (Lewin, 1992b; Varchaver, 1992). Works seized under the shadow of this new ruling have been feminist, lesbian, or gay material, including Marguerite Duras' novella *The Man Sitting in the Corridor* (seized on its way to Trent University), award-winning author David Leavitt's *A Place I've Never Been,* and Albert Innaurato's *Best Plays of Albert Innaurato* which contains the Tony Award winning *Gemini* (Feminist Bookstore News, 1993; Lyall, 1993). *Hothead Paisan*, a lesbian cartoon book, was seized by Canadian customs on its way to Victoria, British Columbia, in 1993. *Hothead Paisan* and *Bad Attitude*, a magazine of lesbian erotica, were seized on their way to Toronto. Two books by Andrea Dworkin, with whom MacKinnon wrote her 1984 anti-pornography law, were seized en route to Montreal (cad, 1993; Feminist Bookstore News, 1993). Booksellers at Toronto's Glad Day Bookshop were indicted on obscenity charges for selling *Bad Attitude* in 1992 (Varchaver, 1992; Gibb, 1992). The store's owner and manager were charged under the section of Canada's criminal code that was the subject of *Butler* and MacKinnon's *amicus* brief.

LABELING: THE EMPEROR'S NEW FIGLEAF

The argument for labeling does not reject the in-depth proposals above but opts for something quicker. Antisocial images abet larger causes of violence, the labeler's reasoning goes. Attacking that piece of the problem will bring some results. Yet under the illusion that labeling is taking care of business, the country is not quick to embark on substantive solutions, as the Clinton Administration's $131 million cut in school drug treatment programs unattractively shows. Perhaps, in judging whether labeling brings even measured relief from violence, the public might look at the industry that has had it for seventy years, through decades of little and much mayhem that it seems not to affect.

"I thought four 'fucks' get you an R—we only had three!" That was Danny DeVito's response when the Motion Picture Association of America (MPAA) gave an R rating to his first directorial effort, *Throw Mama from the Train* (DeVito, 1987). A cleverly written comedy dotted with slapstick, it was intended as a Christmas release for the family audience. DeVito had thought a character could say 'fuck' three times without earning the movie an R. "They gave it a *Fatal Attraction* R. Can't they tell the f---ing difference?"

The "automatic language rule" is one of two firm standards for rating films: In order for a movie to stay clear of an R rating, the word *fuck* can be uttered only once and *only* as an expletive. Thus, saying "Oh fuck, the ratings board is a pain in the . . ." will not trigger an R. But one cannot say, "Fuck the ratings board, it is a pain in the . . ." If the word—or any of the "harsher sexually derived words"—is used as a verb in a sexual context, an R rating is mandated by the MPAA rating guidelines.

The other automatic rule involves drug use: any depiction of marijuana or other drugs (except caffeine, nicotine, or alcohol) requires a PG-13. A depiction lasting more than a little while, as determined by the ratings board, will earn a film an R, even though it may dramatize the damaging effects of drug abuse. *Less Than Zero*, one of the more potent antidrug films of the 1980s, was accordingly given an R rating. (The ratings board may supercede the automatic rules by a three-quarters majority vote and reduce, for example, the rating of a film with two expletives from an R to a PG-13 [Valenti, 1987].)

Outside of sexual language and drugs, there are no precise guidelines for directors or screenwriters, no list of rules quantifying what's suitable for youngsters. Each film is taken as a whole, according to MPAA president Jack Valenti, and evaluated for sex, violence, and "theme" on a case-by-case basis by the Classification and Ratings Association (CARA, an independent division of the MPAA). The CARA board assesses what "most American parents will think about the appropriateness of film content" (Valenti, 1987, p. 9) and then gives the movie a G, PG, PG-13, R, or NC-17 accordingly. The NC-17, introduced in 1991, supplants the X rating which for over twenty years had been used to mark adult themes. (The XXX rating, designating hard-core sex scenes, is given to sexually explicit films by their producers as part of a film's promotion. It is not part of the MPAA system.)

For directors, submitting a film to CARA is a picnic in a minefield. With only broad, descriptive guidelines, directors guess what rating they will get for their footage. DeVito's film tripped the

CARA standards with a reference to a book titled *One Hundred Women I Want to Fuck*. DeVito appealed the ruling but, as he put it, "I had one night in New York and I lost." The book title was changed to *One Hundred Women I Want to Pork,* (which DeVito was not certain showed improvement) and the movie's rating was changed to PG-13. Director David Morris ran into worse trouble with his film *Patti Rocks*. A low budget, feminist take on the relations between men and women, *Patti* got an X not for graphic sex but for explicit language, an industry first. Morris was incredulous and told the MPAA, "I made a film about how men degrade women and now I'm accused of making socially irresponsible material" (Grogg, 1989). Morris and his producer, Sam Grogg, appealed the ruling twice. As part of their defense, they counted the number of F-words in well-known R-rated movies. *Scarface* has 206; *Salvador*, 84; *Beverly Hills Cop 2*, 54; *Full Metal Jacket*, over 30 in the first thirty minutes, when Grogg and Morris stopped counting. *Patti* has 73 (Winer, 1987).

On the second appeal, *Patti* earned just enough votes to get an R. Yet in order to appeal, a director has first to accept the initial rating, which is publicized in the MPAA's weekly bulletin. (The rating is not publicized if the filmmaker intends to cut her film and resubmit a new version to CARA.) "Which means," Grogg pointed out, "that it really messes up your distribution. Most theater chains wouldn't take an X-rated movie, and most newspapers wouldn't advertise it. Even if the appeals board changes the rating, word has gotten around."

The NC-17 rating has given filmmakers and exhibitors a bit of flexibility that is perhaps appropriate to a form that includes *Animal House* and *Last Year at Marienbad*. Whereas many cinemas would not screen an X-rated film (General Cinema, for instance, with over 1,000 theaters nationwide, would not), theater owners often review NC-17 films on a case-by-case basis, unless they are barred by their leases from showing them, as are many located in shopping malls. A good number of video retailers including Blockbuster, the country's largest, will not stock NC-17 films.

Film advertising often faces stiffer criteria. *The New York Times* would not print the title of Stephen Frears's *Sammy and Rosie Get*

Laid, presumably because of the offensive verb. The *Dallas Morning News* rejected an ad for *Patti Rocks* after it won its appeal and got an R. The ad read: "*Patti Rocks* will help you explore an entirely new sexual position . . . honesty." When the paper finally ran the ad, it deleted the word *sexual.*

Unlike books, newspapers, or magazines, motion pictures have operated since the nickelodeon under a system of content regulation. Considered an industry and not a form of expression, movies were extended no protections under the free speech provisions of the First Amendment and were regulated as business ventures. State boards of review looked at each film, marked disagreeable passages for cutting, and when a film passed muster, issued licenses to show it. Barring minors and adults alike from seeing objectionable footage, the licensing procedures acted openly as censorship, as they were intended to. Police and social reformers of the day believed moving pictures corrupted the nation's youth and roused the "immigrant rabble." (For a history of the licensing and rating of motion pictures and court trials of controversial films see *Cinema, Politics and Society in America* edited by Philip Davies and Brian Neve, 1981; *Banned Films: Movies, Censors and the First Amendment* by Edward De Grazia and Roger Newman, 1982; *Film: The Democratic Art* by Garth Jowett, 1976; *Movie-Made America: A Cultural History of American Movies* by Robert Sklar, 1976; *Images of American Life: A History of Ideological Management in Schools, Movies, Radio, and Television* by Joel Spring, 1992; and *The Celluloid Empire: A History of the American Movie Industry* by R. Stanley, 1978.) In 1914, the Pennsylvania code, a model for many other states, proscribed pictures that displayed "nudity, infidelity, women drinking or smoking, or prolonged passion." The Pennsylvania Board of Censors, as it was frankly called, provided a specific definition of "prolonged passion": one yard of celluloid or thirty-six seconds.

During the first five decades of this century, conservative advocacy groups—notably the Catholic Church—applied strong pressure on the federal government not only to maintain state licensing boards but also to establish a national board of censors. Hollywood disliked the idea of a national board. With state regulation there was room for variation in licensing, and a film that was banned in Boston might be shown in Kenosha. Believing that self-regulation would ward off federal review, the major film studios created the Motion Picture Production Code, often referred to as the Hays Code after its first director, William Hays. (*The Censorship Papers: Movie Censorship Letters from the Hays Office, 1934 to 1968,* by Gerald Gardner, offers an overview of the Hays office doings.) The Motion Picture Production Code called the shots in films for over forty years—no code approval, no distribution—and was responsible for the ubiquitous fade-to-black.

Not until 1952, in a dispute over *The Miracle,* by Roberto Rossellini (*Burstyn v. Wilson*), did the Supreme Court rule that film was a "significant medium for the communication of ideas" and so protected by constitutional guarantees of free speech. In the two decades following, the courts ruled in favor of showing contested films in such cases as Otto Preminger's *The Moon Is Blue* (1953), Marc Allegret's *Lady Chatterley's Lover* (1959), Vilgot Sjoman's *I Am Curious—Yellow* (1967), and Mike Nichols's *Carnal Knowledge* (1974). By the late 1960s, the old motion picture code was in shreds on the editing room floor and public concern had shifted from the effect of film on adults to that on minors. In *Ginsberg v. New York* (1968), the Supreme Court ruled that state governments may prohibit minors from seeing material that is legal for adults. In *Interstate Circuit Inc. v. Dallas*, also 1968, the Court found constitutional a Dallas rating system that prohibited sixteen-year-olds from viewing certain films. As in the 1920s, the film industry believed self-regulation would forestall other states from establishing similar rating systems. And so the MPAA wrote the current rating guidelines to "provide *advance information to enable parents* [emphasis original] to make judgments on movies they wanted their children to see or not to see" (Valenti, 1987, p. 4), and in the case of R and X (now NC-17) ratings, to keep minors out of theaters. Prohibitions on admission are enforced by the National Association of Theater Owners. The CARA board has no licensing or police powers; it cannot force a filmmaker to carry a rating or prevent a movie from being shown if the director can find a willing distributor, exhibitor, and advertisers. The ratings do not prevent adults from seeing films.

The proceedings of the ratings system begin when a film is completed and the director submits it to the CARA board. Six to nine people serve on the board, appointed by chair Richard Heffner and approved by MPAA president Jack Valenti. All are parents; they vary in age, religion, ethnicity, and race. The board is anonymous and accountable only to Heffner and the MPAA, which is a private, not a government, organization. After the board screens and rates a film, a filmmaker has three options: she can accept the rating and begin negotiations with distributors, she can re-edit the movie and submit a new version to the CARA board, or she can appeal the decision. The cost of the procedure, paid by the director and producer, varies according to the film's budget and the annual income of the studio that produced it. The fee schedule is the same for MPAA members and independent producers, though the major, wealthier studios pay higher fees. "No one," says board chair Richard Heffner (1989), "has wanted a rating and not gotten one because he or she couldn't afford it."

The appeals board is composed of nine representatives of film studios who are members of the MPAA, eight representatives of the National Association of Theater Owners, four independent members, and Jack Valenti. A two-thirds majority is required to overturn the initial ruling; a simple majority allows the director to appeal again. After the second appeal, the ruling is final. Two other options are open to filmmakers. They can reject the CARA ruling or decline submitting their films for ratings review. They then must apply to distributors with unrated movies, though many theaters will not screen them and, perhaps more important economically, many video stores will not put them on their shelves.

According to *The Voluntary Movie Rating System,* published by the Motion Picture Association of America, the ratings are defined this way (pp. 6–8):

G—"The violence is at a minimum. Nudity and sex scenes are not present; nor is there any drug use content."

PG—"There may be some profanity in these films. There may be violence but it is not deemed so strong that everyone under 17 need be restricted unless accompanied by a parent. Nor is there cumulative horror or violence. . . . There is no drug use content. . . . There is no explicit sex. . . . Brief nudity may appear. . . ."

PG-13—"Any drug use content will initially require at least a PG-13 rating. . . . If nudity is sexually oriented, the film will generally not be found in the PG-13 category. If violence is rough or persistent, the film goes into the R rating. A film's single use of one of the harsher sexually-derived words, though only as an expletive, shall require the Rating Board to issue that film at least a PG-13 rating. More than one such expletive must lead the Rating Board to issue a film an R rating, as must even one of these words used in a sexual context."

R—theaters require that people under 17 be accompanied in the theater by a parent or adult guardian. "The language may be rough, the violence may be hard, drug use content may be included, and while explicit sex is not to be found in R-rated films, nudity and lovemaking may be involved."

NC-17—"No one under 17 admitted. . . . It should be noted, however, that NC-17 does not necessarily mean obscene or pornographic . . . that is for the courts to decide legally. . . . These films may include the accumulation of sexually connected language, or explicit sex, or excessive and sadistic violence."

"We make an educated estimate," CARA board chair Richard Heffner said, "as to what most parents think" (1989; see also Valenti, 1987, p. 9). "It is not clear like in the old days when one nipple was an R, a knife going in was PG, going in and coming out was an R. But the system does have a consistency: we judge films according to what we think most parents feel."

With this, Heffner points to one of CARA's central conundrums. As with books, parents do not agree on what is suitable for minors of difference ages. Yet the eight or so people behind the closed doors of the CARA board are expected to judge an art form for all the families in the country. Perhaps the most disturbing rating is the G. It tells parents they may send their children to such movies without knowing their contents, without worry or supervision. It assures parents that there is nothing on the screen that might "disturb the parent or even the youngest child" (Heffner, 1989; see also Valenti, 1987, p. 6). Wilson, Linz, and Randall (1990) found a good deal of G material that they believe would be troubling for children. The Surgeon General's Workshop (1986) pointed out what most parents know without the expense of a commission: "Children bring individual temperaments and adaptive skills to situations, and the predictability of how particular influences will affect a child is lower than we might expect" (p. 38). It takes more hubris than the Surgeon General's Workshop could muster to impose CARA's judgments on the country through nationwide ratings that are affixed to a work of art or entertainment (not published separately in an organizational bulletin that interested audiences may obtain) and that in two cases, the R and NC-17, carry power over admissions that supercedes parental judgment.

Ratings have for many parents the appeal of the short cut. Without seeing a film, one knows what is suitable for one's child: no G, no go. One knows, for example, that Dan Aykroyd's comedy *The Couch Trip*, Adrian Lyne's thriller *Fatal Attraction*, and Oliver Stone's war film *Platoon* are all Rs, all the same. The V rating on television programs will likewise mark *N.Y.P.D. Blue,* a drama about rape, and one about the Passion, a bloody story if ever there was one. More information about movies can be gleaned from their advertisements, where sex and violence are noted as selling points.

Adults often disagree with critics, who disagree with each other and who back their opinions with columns of print. Yet the ratings system suggests that parents trust a single letter. The MPAA has considered over the years recommendations to expand the ratings from a letter to a phrase such as "moderately offensive language" only to find the problems redoubled. To some, off-color expletives are offensive, to others, government war boosting is. To some, screen homosexuality is a problem, to others, homophobia.

Designating a theme as criterion for movie ratings gives credence to those who dislike it. The MPAA rates sex, for instance, but not sexism. In solving the problem of whose dislikes shall govern, majority opinion does not suffice. A majority of Americans regularly use four-letter words, yet one off-color verb mandates an R. A majority of Americans hold racial prejudices in subtle or robust ways, yet the MPAA would not rate movies for the presence of black people or interracial marriages.

Other problems with the ratings system present themselves. What began as parental advice often becomes sales promotion. Directors insert and snip footage to a recipe that will earn them the rating that will attract the most viewers. Conventional wisdom is that the most profitable rating is the R. According to the MPAA, in 1991, 375 films (61 percent) were rated R; in 1992 the figure was up to 390 films (63.3 percent). One might have wondered why "penis breath" is in the script of Steven Spielberg's otherwise innocuous *E.T.* It boosted the rating to a PG; not even grammar schoolers want to sit through a G.

The rating system is at times more restrictive than government censorship. Current obscenity law respects community differences, recognizing that what is acceptable in Pumpkin Patch may not be in Newark. The MPAA takes no regard of community standards and believes it can reasonably assess what most American parents think across the country. The rating system also impedes parental wishes more than government. According to harmful-to-minors law, legislatures and courts may rule that minors are prohibited from buying what adults may. But government may not prevent parents from purchasing and showing their children such material, should they wish. Yet a mother cannot send her sixteen-year-old daughter to see Wayne Wang's *The Joy Luck Club*, a story about Chinese-American mothers and daughters based on the best-selling novel by Amy Tan. *The Joy Luck Club* is rated R and requires that minors be accompanied in the theater by a parent or guardian. In a stranger case, the teenage star of *Medium Cool* (1969, rated R) could not get into a theater to see it. Nor could a mother accompany her teenager to see Philip Kaufman's lacy *Henry & June*, based on the writings of Anaïs Nin, or Bernardo Bertolucci's *Last Tango in Paris*. These films were rated NC-17 and X respectively, which bar all people under the age of 17, including those accompanied by parents.

Lastly, the ratings system exceeds the law by its subjective stan-

dards. CARA chair Richard Heffner said, "One film will have a nipple, another film won't, and both will get a PG because we think the
films *qua* films are PG" (Heffner, 1989). It is difficult to imagine that
Henry & June would be legally harmful to minors, or to anything save
Nin's reputation. Government could not prevent teenagers from
seeing it or reading a book based on its screenplay. Yet the ratings
system overrides both law and parents with the NC-17 and keeps
those under seventeen out of theaters. Lois Scheinfeld (New York
University) wrote in *Film Comment* (1986), "The MPAA's assertion
that its ratings are necessary to fend off government censorship is
simply disingenuous; the MPAA has not met the enemy, but instead
has given away what the enemy lacks the power to take" (p. 11).

The MPAA could remedy the problem of subjectivity with lists of
acts permissible in each rating category, much as the Hays Code
had—and for which it was ruled unconstitutional for violating protections against prior restraint. (To prevent secret trials and ensure
the public's access to controversial material, government may not
ban a work from circulation before it has been published or exhib-
ited.) As a result, the MPAA may not dictate in advance what a filmmaker must include or excise from a film to fit a rating. In sum, the
old Hays code ran afoul of free speech principles because it was too
narrow or prescriptive; today's rating system runs afoul of them because it is too broad.

Ironically, in spite of its problems of subjectivity, the MPAA today cuts close enough to prior restraint. Though the ratings are
technically voluntary, a wrong rating mangles distribution. Filmmakers take their "indications," as Sam Grogg (1989) called it, from
the ratings board, and cut their movies. This makes the rating system one of voluntary prior restraint, or self-censorship. Standard
film contracts between studios and directors regularly require filmmakers to deliver movies edited to earn the ratings that the marketing department wants. The MPAA goes further than the studios. "If
a filmmaker asks why he got a certain rating," said Heffner (1989),
"we tell him as specifically as we can. If he wants to re-edit the thing
and submit a new version, we have to look at it, even if he comes
back eight times—which we've done. We prefer that directors don't
edit. We prefer that they go out with the rating, or unrated."

"Sure he prefers it," Grogg said, "it's not his pocketbook."

According to Heffner, directors cut and resubmit "a lot of times. I can't say what percent but a substantial amount." By comparison, the number of filmmakers who keep their films intact and appeal the rating is "comparatively few—maybe a half-dozen or dozen a year."

SOME OF THE RULES SOME OF THE TIME

- A few seconds of Mickey Rourke's derrière were removed from the lovemaking scene in *Angel Heart* to reduce the rating from X to R. A year earlier, Rob Lowe's bum bobbing atop Demi Moore was okayed in *About Last Night*. *Angel Heart* includes a fair amount of violence and, in the lovemaking scene, surreal images of blood dripping from the ceiling. Some may find this bizarre or offensive, but it is not clear how bun-paring remedies matters. Since Rourke's bottom is proscribed, perhaps the next time a Rourke vehicle calls for a nude scene, the producers will ask Lowe to stand—or lie—in.
- The exploitation film *Class of 1984* had a difficult time reducing its rating from an X to an R. Finally, the director cut three hip undulations, transforming one passage from a five-hump sex scene to a two-hump one.
- More buttock trouble: Fassbinder's last movie, the hothouse art film *Querelle*, contains homosexual acts, Brad Davis's privates clearly outlined through his underpants, and "the whole set is arguably an erect penis," one company executive put it. In one scene, shot above the waist, Davis has anal intercourse with another man. One sees the fellow spit into his hand to lubricate himself and one sees him bearing down behind Davis. When the MPAA asked for a cut, it was of the smile on Davis's face when the men were done.

(continued)

SOME OF THE RULES SOME OF THE TIME (*cont.*)

- In *Crimes of Passion*, the set designer had the misjudgment to decorate Kathleen Turner's apartment with Aubrey Beardsley prints that contain male nudity. The prints, the originals of which hang in museums open to the public, had to go.

- *The Last Emperor*, Bertolucci's sumptuous film about the history of twentieth-century China, contains two naked breasts in a wet-nurse scene, a few seconds of an implied lesbian liaison, one or two seconds of a graphic death scene, and some opium usage. Columbia Pictures wanted a PG-13 and worried about the lesbianism, the graphic death, and possibly the breasts. The opium turned out to be the problem, though it destroys the lives of those who use it and sends a clear antidrug message. Columbia's response to the MPAA: this is a history film, you've got to be kidding.

- In the bubbly family film *Murphy's Romance*, Sally Field's onscreen ex-husband asks her new boyfriend (James Garner), "Are you fucking Emma?" "If I were," Garner answers, "I wouldn't use that word." The one F-word in a sexual context earned the film an R, though the point of the scene is that the word is nasty and should not be used. The scene was rewritten.

- Some filmmakers suspect that the automatic language rule makes no contribution to the country's moral health and have challenged it in their scripts. When Dustin Hoffman and Warren Beatty finally best the bad guys in *Ishtar*, Hoffman shouts at them, "Fuck you." Beatty was also supposed to shout, but rumor has it that for his whole career Beatty had wanted to say "fuck" two times in a movie without getting an R. To the bad guys in *Ishtar* he said "Fuck you twice" and got away with it.

The performance of the movie rating system suggests it is more restrictive than government censorship, manipulates filmmakers not only for what they take out of films but for what they put in and is better for marketing than education. Linz, Wilson, and Donnerstein wrote (1992), "The criticisms voiced by the general public indicate that the application of ratings to certain films may be at best uninformative and at worst misleading" (p. 154). Advocates of TV labeling suggest it will not share these movie industry problems because TV ratings will rate only violence. Disregarding the tendency of systems to enlarge themselves, one might nevertheless be skeptical. The greatest complaint against the 1993 TV labeling proposal was timidity; most labeling advocates hope for the rapid adoption of a comprehensive, detailed system. Terry Rakolta, head of Americans for Responsible Television, and William Abbott, president of the Foundation to Improve Television, both called the 1993 labels "tepid." Senator Edward Markey continued to push for the TV chip that automatically blocks all programming labeled V (violence) (Andrews, 1993a; 1993b; O'Connor, 1993). Additionally, the difficulties that filmmakers face with distributors and advertisers will repeat themselves with TV networks, cable companies, and advertisers. In practice this means that *The Accused*, a powerful antirape film starring Jody Foster and Kelly McGillis, would be rated V on the TV labeling system. A cable company or network that wished to screen the film might find it could not attract advertisers for it or that "decency" groups might threaten a boycott. A likely result is that the film would not be aired.

Wilson, Linz, and Randall (1990) proposed another rating system that identifies film content more specifically than does the MPAA. It includes the categories Horror, Violence, Sex, and Sex and Violence, and the age groups 3–7, 8–12 and 13–17. The Wilson et al. system reflects their concern not only with images that may teach youngsters nasty behavior but also with those that might frighten them. The authors place *The Wizard of Oz* in the Horror category for the 3–7 age group. MPAA president Jack Valenti has called content specific proposals "a logistical nightmare. If it says V, [the moviegoer] wants to know what kind of violence . . . to what degree, in what detail" (Mathews, 1987).

Valenti has nabbed the beast. Viewers want to know precisely the content of a TV program or film so they may judge its suitability for their children. Some parents find violence repellant unless the military does it, others, especially when the military does it. Unless one group submits to the other, the reasonable solution is a personalized rating system, which film advertisements are in many ways and which Stuart Klawans, film critic at *The Nation,* recommend. "All ratings," he says, "should be PG" (Klawans, 1994). Peggy Charren, founder of Action for Children's Television, proposes that a device be affixed to TV sets like the one that lets viewers record individual programs onto videocassettes. It would allow parents to screen out individual programs to suit their children's needs; the technology needed to do this is currently available. "Congress should mandate," she writes (Charren, 1993), "that every set carry a computer connection that permits parents to lock out shows they consider inappropriate for their kids. With 500 available channels around the corner, it makes sense to build into TV sets a programmable capability that scrambles unwanted signals." About the V blocking chip she says, "To enable viewers to cancel categories of programs puts too much control in the hands of those applying the ratings."

Supporters of the V rating and blocking chip argue that an effective system must block V-rated programs categorically because some parents will not check programs on a case-by-case basis. Perhaps, but parents who do not attend to their children's reading and viewing likely do not attend to them in more basic ways. If public policy fails to address parental neglect, TV labeling will be of little consequence. In August 1993, the National Medical Association representing 16,000 black physicians convened a special session on reducing violence in the African-American community. According to association president Leonard Lawrence, they discussed not TV but poverty, poor schooling, racism, drug and alcohol abuse, the availability of guns, and the need "to teach youngsters the positive aspects of discipline at a very early age, teaching them how to achieve, how to learn, how to interact with other people" (Herbert, 1993a).

Nine

THE RETURN OF THE IRREPRESSIBLE
Sex Scares and Witch Hunts

A s a proposal for life's improvement, image-blaming has several charms to its advantage. For one, it offers the boost of activism. Sexual and violent images are visible, tinged with the illicit, and far easier to expunge than deeply rooted injustices. Well-meaning citizens believe they can fight them, beat them, and win. Effectiveness is an important emotion, especially to Americans with their famous can-do mentality. Perhaps inherited from the frontier culture, it holds that something can be done about everything, now. Feminists are exhausted fighting a sexist economy and politics, and sexual violence. Most Americans are at a loss in a difficult economy and in the face of rapid changes in gender, family, and race relations. The "decency" movements are a boon to many people who want to control their lives (Pally, 1985a, b). In this, they have the same appeal as the sexual and violent fantasies they assail. Casting words and images as bad guys or bad mommies, image blaming provides a frightening but beatable monster and the pledge of a happy ending. As long as life is insecure, this pledge will have a market. Like monster, gangster or sex films, image-blaming is a myth that sells.

Psychologist Paula Webster suggests another idea. She writes that image blaming feels right because it carries "the voice of mom" (Webster, 1985). Most people in Western societies grow up with the feeling that sex is icky and abandon, dangerous. Most women grow up with the assurance that men are dangerous. However adults traffic in the sexual aspects of life, these messages remain embedded in the imagination and emotional core. Dr. Martin Klein (1992) writes, "Kids learn that sex is bad. . . . Children know that they are sexual, so they conclude that they are bad. Unconsciously, they fear being abandoned or destroyed because of their sexuality. This is not a *metaphorical* fear—for young children, dependent on the caretaking and good will of their parents, it is a *literal* fear. In terror, kids learn to hide, deny, repress, and distort their sexuality. Using a familiar process we call internalization or introjection, children take over the life-and-death job of scrutinizing their sexuality from their parents" (p. 2).

When one is told in one's adult years that sexual imagery is dirty and makes men dangerous, it "clicks." The "truths" absorbed in childhood and recast in adult language sound infallible. Heard indirectly or point blank, they have become a lens through which one sees the world. But they need not have been heard at all. Biology, with fear and anger whipped into sexual desire, makes sex suspect. Human beings will ever be wary of sex and blame it for an array of ills. Suspicion of sex is the universal culprit and oldest quick fix in the Western tradition. Wary of dark nights and writhing, one calls them *Walpurgisnacht* and blames the witches for one's woes—the women in the short skirts, videos, or posters on the wall.

LACE STRINGS AND BRUTES:
THE CONFINING PLEASURES OF THE VICTIM

Image blaming has special appeal for women. It embellishes the stance of victim, a state of mind and heart that has for women the comforts of familiarity and flattery. Under image blaming, women are victimized not only by sexist and violent action but by "dirty" words. In 1992–93, some feminists began describing the emotional and tactical uses of the cult of the victim, as some have called it (De Crow, 1993; Lewin, 1992c; Roiphe, 1993a, 1993b; Young, 1992). They risked blurring violence against women with wolf-calling and blaming the victim, and they angered many women. Yet they turned attention to one of the last gilded cages of femininity remaining since Betty Friedan banged at the bars of *The Feminine Mystique* thirty years ago.

Like all disenfranchised groups, women have used whatever they could to gain control over their lives, however minimally. They have had little choice over their tactics; most often women have had to turn to their advantage what men believe about them. These are the manipulations of the powerless. If men think women frail and male egos are boosted by protecting them, the pride and prejudices of men may be enlisted on women's behalf. If one cannot act on one's own behalf, as women for so long could not, this may be the best route to go. If it is legal to beat one's wife with a stick, as it was till the nineteenth century, women are wise to be so fragile as to deserve male protection. Where women may not leave the house without the permission of fathers or husbands, women are wise to be so gentle and refined that men feel obliged to behave well at home. The advantage for women is that they gain influence over their world; female delicacy has claims on male behavior where women's rights do not. Daughters have for generations learned these wisdoms in varying forms from their mothers. The manipulations of the powerless are the bedrock of girl training, and they will be longer in changing than the laws on suffrage, gender discrimination, and family leave.

Women's expectations for power, to be hired and heard as men are, have rarely been greater than they are in industrialized countries today. Yet social change creeps, and it is little wonder that women dig around for something that will make a difference now—especially American women, as hooked as American men on the quick fix. Subtle and overt sexism persists in public and private spheres, and women know in a collective unconscious of sorts that delicacy, wooed properly, brings control. The world does not yet treat women fairly; women are tired of working all day and picking up socks at night. Wouldn't they like to be treated like ladies again?

Rape accounts for 0.7 percent of crimes against persons; 0.4 percent are attempted, 0.3 percent completed. Older white women are twenty times less likely than young black men to be victims of violent crime (Reiss & Roth, 1993, pp. 4, 58). Yet Katie Roiphe (1993a, b) writes about the "rape culture" on college campuses as sequestering "feminism in a teary province of trauma and crisis. By blocking analysis with its claims to unique pandemic suffering, the rape crisis becomes a powerful source of authority" (p. 28). It is the authority that counts. Male students still get more attention in class; they are only a little less sexist than their fathers. But victims of pandemic rape get heard.

The cult of victim offers other benefits as well. A campus dating code that, as Roiphe writes (p. 28), "not only dictates the way sex *shouldn't be* but also the way it *should* be" soothes the emotional conflicts of young women who want to have sex but were not brought up to take it for themselves. The lessons of sexual danger and female propriety linger still. In a *Village Voice* roundtable on college women and sex (Rosier, 1993), one woman said, "Women want to go out and have a good time, but because of what's been drummed into our heads for years about being more passive, that you've got to have sex with romantic love, people feel guilty. A lot of women are apprehensive about just going out and scoring theirs" (p. 34). Date rape handbooks in which men are rapacious and women resisting echo fears learned in girlhood about sex and men. They "click" and comfort. Roiphe writes about the campus culture of *Clarissa*, (1991a, b), whose fall from innocence Samuel Richardson detailed at length. One might also remember *Moll Flanders*, one of the greatest passiveaggressives in literature till she donned men's clothes and learned how to steal.

Cathy Young writes about *surgical rape* (1992, p. 20), a term used to identify women who have had abortions as the victims of abortionists. Tamar Lewin (1992c) writes of antipornography feminists who have "joined with conservatives seeking a return to traditional values." A Northwestern University law professor proposed in 1993 that cities make illegal men's comments to women on the street because they "inhibit a woman's ability to walk in public places, threaten her sense of security and can serve as a precursor to rape. People ask me why I want to work on a problem that is considered trivial when there are other problems like rape and domestic violence. My response is that this is a piece of that violence" (A Move to Protect Women, 1993). Street comments may be annoying or vile, but calling them violence turns an inconvenience into a danger and makes women afraid. Rather than take back the night, victim-thinking gives it over to the bad guys and hopes the sheriff comes to the rescue. It gives to men power they could not fully get for themselves. Traditionally men have wanted to control women and so kept women weak. But women found ways to subvert them. Today, women victim-thinkers make themselves frail and seek male "care." In 1993, the city of Toronto, supported by a number of feminist groups, considered a bill that would make illegal all sexual material in the city—including nonobscene works and those made by and for women. Borrowing from workplace harassment codes, the bill's authors submitted that the presence of sexual material, even in opaque covers behind blinder racks, constitutes a "hostile environment" for female residents.

Workplace harassment law is the mother of victim politics. What began as a much-needed remedy to unwanted touching, rape, and the *quid pro quo* requirement of sexual favors in return for job or promotion has become in some quarters a war against Miss March, compliments, sexual innuendo, and jokes. With Anita Hill's testimony at the Clarence Thomas Supreme Court confirmation hearings in 1991, sexual harassment became a new single issue for American women. Much in the workplace remains unfair—the glass ceiling, pay inequities, and the ways in which men's voices have still, to men and women both, greater weight. Women may not yet be able to redress these, but they may keep men from using "dirty" words. At least one will have done something, if only a sad reprise of washing boys' mouths out with soap. The women who policed "foul language" in their homes knew they had little control over their male children and less over their husbands. But it was a moment when they could exact their will. The women of the Christian Temperance Union knew they had little say over their husband's drinking and less over their drunken violence. But smashing demon rum must have felt superb.

In 1993, Feminists for Free Expression (FFE), a national nonprofit anticensorship organization, filed an *amicus* brief to the Supreme Court in the case of *Harris v. Forklift Systems, Inc*. FFE suggested a sexual harassment standard that would prohibit workplace intimidation and assault without relying on "unspoken and counter-productive assumptions about women—that women are indeed the 'weaker sex' and cannot survive in the workplace unless it is cleansed of all banter and expression about sexuality. These assumptions fundamentally disserve women, perpetuating gender-based stereotypes of both men and women, but particularly of women as fragile, asexual beings whose delicate sensibilities require special protection" (Feminists for Free Expression, 1993, p. 5). FFE recommended that unwanted touching, *quid pro quo* sexual favors, and targeted, repeated verbal harassment be considered to create a hostile work environment, but not the possession or display of sexual material or sexual banter.

Assumptions of female fragility are so embedded in sexual harassment law that regulations are overinclusive of sexual speech that is not harassing and underinclusive of harassing speech that is not sexual. "Semantic confusion has led to doctrinal confusion," wrote Cathy Crosson, author of the FFE brief (p. 15). As 'sex' in English means both the erotic activity and gender, sexual harassment has come to mean abuse by erotic material rather than because of one's gender. A supervisor who feels threatened by women on the job and taunts them for being "slow" is likely more harassing than one who tells an off-color joke at the water cooler. Yet sexual harassment law does not cover his taunts because the language is not sexual.

Sexual harassment will not be solved by lists of nasty words or pictures that offend women, the "reasonable woman" as the courts sometimes try to define her, or women as a class. Except in cases of assault, *quid pro quos,* and targeted verbal harassment, sexual harassment will not be remedied by law. Women are not discomfited by the same material, and lists of proscribed words will prompt men reasonably to ask if not "What do women want?" then "What does each and every woman at every job I've had want?" A more effective solution: look at her. If a man makes a remark to a woman once and she squirms, it is a mistake. He cannot be expected to have read her mind. If he makes the remark again, he does it to make her squirm, and that is unacceptable by standards of good management and manners. Men are not dulled to the nuances of gesture and conversation. They are keen to every detail of one-upmanship, turf jousting, and allegiance in the workplace, and every note of love and petulance at home. To address the problem of sexual harassment, one need address why men want to make women squirm. That is a matter for personnel offices, workplace education programs, and all manner of public discussion that makes people better see themselves and others. It is a matter of that slow beast, cultural change.

Crosson's protest against "weaker sex" thinking in workplace harassment law echoes Roiphe's against the campus culture of rape. Citing college codes that consider "verbal coercion" rape, Roiphe notes they draw women as naive know-nothings and men as the stronger sex, intellectually and emotionally. (Verbal coercion is "verbal arguments not including verbal threats of force," 1993a, p. 30). Roiphe quotes Catharine MacKinnon's well-known phrase, " 'Politically, I call it rape whenever a woman has sex and feels violated'," and then writes, "The language of virtue and violation reinforces retrograde stereotypes. . . . In one woman's account of date rape in the *Rag,* a feminist magazine at Harvard, she talks about the anguish of being 'defiled.' Another writes, 'I long to be innocent again.' With such anachronistic constructions of the female body, with all their assumptions about female purity, these young women frame their experience of rape in archaic sexist terms" (p. 30).

Conservative columnist Mona Charren put it frankly: "In a twin-kling of an eye (a male eye), women abandoned the standards of sex-ual conduct which had protected them from untempered male lust for millennia" only to "look at their hands and recognize that they had given away their trump" (Young, 1992, p. 20–21). Each woman who strays from good-girl propriety, who gives away the milk for free as the saying goes, lessens the chance that men will buy the cow. She threatens the security of other women. In a world where women were economically dependent on men, they were wise to be so rare a commodity that men would pay for them. They were wise to check the commodity's supply and police other women's chastity. Today's victim culture polices women as well into herds of ladies joined in timorousness. The trouble with don't-give-the-milk-for-free thinking is that women must think of themselves as cows. "In-dividual identity," writes Young, "becomes replaced by a group identity based on victimhood: if a woman does not perceive herself as a victim, she can no longer speak for women and is no longer seen as speaking in an 'authentically female' voice" (p. 23).

For Karen De Crow, NOW past president, the cult of victim is the worst sort of return of the repressed. It is the comeback of the bad old days she built feminism to forget. She writes, "What we had in mind 25 years ago was not a new puritanism, but freeing women from being eternal children. As grown-ups we have won the right to say no, and be believed and taken seriously. We also have the right to repeat, after Molly Bloom, 'Yes I said yes I will yes'." De Crow believes this born-again puritanism hobbles female sexuality and does not see its appeal to young women. Yet it appeals as do other forms of image blaming: it lures with the boosts of activism and the quick fix, the deep comforts of childhood myths reprised, and the warmth of community. "It is easy," writes Young, "to persuade some people to see themselves as victims because, after all, is there anyone who does not feel he or she has been sometimes treated un-fairly? Blaming it on sexism—or on women's liberation—can make it seem easier somehow, less arbitrary and more remediable; one's suffering can even be dignified by making it a political cause. Denouncing the unfairness of life—let alone taking a hard look at some of your own decisions that may have contributed to your unhappiness—is far less appealing than denouncing men, or feminists, or both" (p. 23).

As an atavistic survival strategy and relief from the responsibilities of adulthood, victim-thinking is deeply attractive. As a source of sexual thrills, it is even more so. Imagining themselves the victims of "verbal coercion," the *Maja Desnuda* or ever-imminent date rape, women steal for themselves the fantasy of ravishment. Victim culture is the college girl's Harlequin romance. Like all fantasies, it distinguishes itself from reality. Rape is not titillating; the culture of rape is. It is in many ways the ideal female fantasy, allowing women abandon while sparing them agency and ensuring their purity. Clarissa lost her innocence, was raped, and died miserably. Girls who read *Clarissa* get off.

The sexual and economic revolution that De Crow wanted could not be accomplished in the generation between herself and Katie Roiphe. In women's emotional core, where motive begins, sex is still icky and soils them; men are still dangerous and need be cajoled. The manipulations of the powerless are ways to broker such a world. But they also keep women in it. When women must resist, they cannot do sex—for good or evil, it must be done to them. They cannot have taken too much drink or bedded a man casually. They certainly cannot have bedded him though the guy was a bad idea and the sex worse. They cannot make a mistake. Feeling soiled by "icky" sex, women feel they have been raped. Women are indeed coerced, bullied, and raped by their dates. National crimes statistics find that women are more often abused by men they know than by strangers. This is problem enough; the new victim culture creates other ones. It recasts a woman who has acted on her own and disliked the evening's end into a creature who cannot act or recover from bad evenings. It takes a woman who agreed to sex because she wanted to be nice or loving or because she worried she'd be thought a bitch if she didn't—and it bolsters the very "femininity" that encouraged her uncomfortable agreement. There are no statistics on how often women do this, but the culture of victim teaches women they should.

Image blaming, which casts women as victims of words and pictures, is another manipulation of the powerless. Like female frailty, it identifies the many things from which women must be guarded and lays claims to male protection. It too "clicks" when recast in modern language. Roiphe notes that today's victim cultists do not talk of "shame" but of "post traumatic stress syndrome." The student writing to the *Rag* was more honest and wrote of being "defiled." Where loss of chastity cost a woman not only a husband but often all social cover, women were wise to be very chaste. Yet chastity, like delicacy and unworldliness, advances a world where women must be dolls. The "wisdoms" that women have learned for protection betray them. Manipulations of the powerless keep women so.

Image-blaming, sexual and nonsexual, will not prevent rape or drug wars, nor will it fell sexism. It has no business being the basis for legislative or judicial remedies to discrimination or violence. Ted Bundy grew up in a home so violent he put butcher knives in his bed at age three. But "pornography made him do it." Fifty-two percent of the most violent juvenile offenders have family who have also been in prison. But TV made them do it. The parents of two teenagers who committed suicide claimed rock made them do it. To prove their point and collect monetary compensation, the parents went to court, where other information about the boys came to light. Ray Belknap was 18; his parents separated before he was born. His mother married four times and her last husband regularly beat Ray. He also threatened Ray's mother with a gun in front of the boy, according to police. Ray had quit high school after two years and was a heavy user of hallucinogens and cocaine. But the rock group Judas Priest made him do it. James Vance, Ray's friend, was born when his mother was 17. She beat him when he was a child and when he got older, he beat her in return. He also had a history of drug abuse and boasted of drinking two six-packs of beer a day. But the lyrics made him do it (Quindlen, 1990).

The court decided against Ray and James's parents, ruling that Judas Priest could not be considered the cause of their suicides (Band is Held Not Liable, 1990). Would that the cure to society's troubles were a matter of eliminating rock, pornography, or "bad" TV. Neither rape, racism, street violence, nor sexism are so single-issue or so easy. Attorney and writer Stephen Rohde wrote (1991), "Suppressing racist speech will not eliminate racism. Suppressing sexist speech will not abolish sexism. Suppressing anti-gay speech will not eradicate homophobia. Admittedly, suppression does give momentary respite to those who suffer the sting of hateful epithets, and it does convey an institutional opposition to bigotry. But these are short-lived benefits achieved at high cost. Not only are the delicate, vital values of free speech seriously jeopardized, but suppression inevitably creates a climate of thought control, a habit of censorship and an atmosphere of reactionary conformity, none of which advances the real goals of eliminating discrimination, promoting diversity and building a pluralist society" (p. 24).

Censorship has always been more problem than solution. It purges society of books, movies, and music, leaving hate, racism, sexism, drug abuse, poverty, and violence flourishing as they did before the printing press and movie camera. It flatters the nation into thinking it has done something to better life while it ignores what might be done.

Ten

SAY IT AGAIN, SAM
Responding to Offensive Speech

IN THE BEGINNING WAS THE WORD: HATE SPEECH AND UNIVERSITY CAMPUSES

Responding to offensive or dangerous speech is an unresolved problem that has been, since the mid-1980s, debated vigorously on university campuses. Two proposals frame the discussion: that the answer to "bad" speech is, in the words of Justice Brandeis, "more speech"; and that the anwer to "bad" speech is hate speech codes. The proponents of campus speech codes argue that "hate speech" is not expression protected by the First Amendment but rather an act that calls up past and present systems of oppression, carries the threat of intimidation or violence, wounds women and minority students, and keeps them from enjoying equal access to education. Universities are obliged, according to speech code advocates, to define prohibited language and punish those who use it. Proponents of "more speech" suggest that speech restrictions are misguided for reasons of ethics and tactics. They make one's opponents martyrs of censorship and establish principles under which one's ideas may next be banned, a particularly bitter outcome for women and minorities. On this view, "bad" speech is best used as an occasion to attract attention to "better" speech, to open that edifying thing, debate. Thomas Paine wrote, "He that would make his own liberty secure, must guard even his enemy from opposition; for if he violates this duty, he establishes a precedent that will reach to himself." The tough part about free speech is enduring it when the other guy is talking.

By 1991, 60 percent of American college campuses had written hate speech policies and another 11 percent were considering them (Rohde, 1991). In 1993 the University of Pennsylvania, a leader in campus speech governance, declared itself an "open expression" campus, with "monitors" to ensure that speech is "open," as the administration sees it (Yardley, 1993). The legal theory behind campus speech codes was developed in the 1980s by a group of professors including Richard Delgado, who helped the University of Wisconsin adopt its well-known hate speech code in 1989 and coauthored (with Mari Matsuda, Charles Lawrence III, and Kimberle Williams Crenshaw) *Words That Wound: Critical Race Theory, Assaultive Speech, and the First Amendment*.

At the University of Wisconsin, what began as a bar to harassing conduct against women and minorities ended as a ban, however well-intentioned, on select words. The campus speech code provided university disciplinary measures against any student who made "racist or discriminatory comments, epithets or other expressive behavior . . . if such comments . . . intentionally (a) demean the race, sex, religion, color, creed, disability, sexual orientation, national origin, ancestry or age of the individual or individuals; and (b) create an intimidating, hostile or demeaning environment for education, university related work, or other university-authorized activity."

The code became famous for permitting overbroad application. One student who stole a roommate's bank card was found guilty of racial discrimination and put on probation because the roommate was Japanese (Bernstein, 1993).

In 1991, the Wisconsin code was ruled unconstitutional for overbroad content-based prohibitions against speech. Delgado and others continue to develop "critical race theory" and to craft hate speech restrictions they hope will pass constitutional muster. In 1993, Delgado and Jean Stefancic published their article "Overcoming Legal Barriers to Regulating Hate Speech on Campus," where they wrote, "hateful speech is not a symptom of subordination (as it is often thought to be) but its very source. . . . it wounds the victim while conveying no valid information" (pp. B1–B2). Delgado and Stefancic do not say in their article where hateful speech comes from. One concludes they mean it is the root of and precedes other forms of prejudice, a strangely literary view of human motive and social structures. Stranger still, Delgado and Stefancic claim that "hate speech" is at once without information (so nothing is lost when it is censored) and potent enough to wound. Far from containing no information, "hate speech" contains a good deal of it, much of it political, which is why Delgado and Stefancic dislike it. As for whether that information is valid, the speaker no doubt thinks it is as valid as Delgado and Stefancic believe their words to be. Appeal to majority opinion to resolve the issue would not serve Delgado and Stefancic well, as most Americans would not endorse their views, even those who agree that racism is wrong. To safeguard their proposals, the authors rely on First Amendment protections of unpopular speech. In sum, the ideas of racists—held to be invalid by Delgado and Stefancic—retain a place in the debate on racism by the very principle that allows the ideas of Delgado and Stefancic—considered invalid by others in the debate—to retain their place.

Other contradictions in the critical race theory present themselves. Stanford professor Thomans Grey, one of the authors of that campus's speech code, maintains that university administrations do not fulfill their obligations to women and minorities until they go beyond condemning hate speech and punish it. His position is supported by most critical race theorists: the words of a university are insufficient to combat prejudice and need be supported by action. "Why is it 'mere words,'" asked Henry Louis Gates Jr. (1993) of Grey's thinking, "when a university only condemns racist speech, but not 'mere words' that the student utters in the first place? Whose words are 'only words'? Why are racist words deeds [not protected by free speech principles], but anti-racist words just lip service?" (p. 43). Gates notes another contradiction of hate speech codes: "We are told that victims of racist speech are cured—that is, empowered—when they learn they are 'not alone' in their subordination, but subordinated as a group. But elsewhere we are told that what makes racist speech peculiarly wounding is that it conveys precisely the message that you are a member of a subordinated group. How can the suggestion of group subordination be the poison *and* the antidote?" (p. 46, emphasis original). Gates's question recalls the writings of Katie Roiphe and Cathy Young about the victim cult among campus feminists, and might be asked of those who promote it.

Mari Matsuda, coauthor of *Words That Wound*, proposes that racism is universally condemned, unlike many political positions that may be argued back and forth and are protected by the First Amendment, and that society is obliged to express its condemnation in its laws. She also holds that racist epithets take power from their link to a prevailing system of racist structures. These two propositions make one knot. If racism is everywhere rebuked, campus codes slay windmills. If it is a prevailing political doctrine worth fighting, it must be protected by free speech principles if any political views are to be safe. The alternative is to have a committee decide the political views in favor, which might make even Matsuda worry that she would not get on it. Matsuda's contradiction points to an unpleasant assumption of critical race theorists: that hate speech codes are permissible because they reflect majority opinion. Setting aside Matsuda's naive views about racism's disrepute, one wonders what should become of minority views, like the many Matsuda holds.

These problems aside, several campuses discovered that hate speech codes backfire against the groups they were designed to protect. Like the antipornography statute in Canada that led to the indictment against woman-made erotica and to the customs confiscation of the works of antipornography activist Andrea Dworkin, hate speech codes are not infrequently used against minority students. In the eighteen months that the University of Michigan applied its speech code, black students were accused of racist speech in over twenty cases (Gottlieb, 1990). Students were punished twice under the code's anti-racist provisions, both times for speech by or on behalf of blacks (Strossen, 1990). Investigations of speech regulations internationally have found similar results (Coliver, 1992).

Delgado and Stefancic (1993) recommend two sorts of speech regulations they believe will conform to Constitutional requirements of free specch. One would increase penalties for campus offenses if they were motivated by bias. The second would penalize "severe, disruptive insults"; the example Delgado and Stefancic give is "you incompetent illiterate fool" (p. B2). The insult prohibition, Delgado and Stefancic concede, would need be racially neutral (presumably neutral as to gender, ethnicity, religion, age, physical status, and sexual orientation as well), so that a student who called another an "asshole" could be hauled off to the dean. Whatever this may do for minorities, it casts the university *in loco parentis*, which students just a few years ago fought mightily against. "Few imagined," Gates (1993) wrote of speech code supporters, "that the restrictions would lead to substantive rights or minority empowerment. They just believed that gutter epithets violate the sort of civility that ought to prevail on campus. In spirit, then, the new regulations were little different from the rules about curfews, drinking or the after-hours presence of women in male dormitories that once governed America's campuses" (p. 46).

More critically, Delgado and Stefancic (1993) do not explain how such intervention will benefit students. How will university-wide bans on "asshole" fell racism? They write that it will bring equality and that "speech without equality is a hollow illusion" (p. B3). But one cannot get equality from protectionism; one can only protect one's role as victim. Delgado, Stefancic, Matsuda et al. create a culture of the victim as surely as do right-wing feminists. As with the women's victim cult, minority victim culture is flattering and famil-iar—flattering because, as blameless victims, minorities need not look into their own conduct, and familiar because enlisting the pro-tection of the master of the house is something women and minori-ties know well how to do. Yet those who so maneuver lose their chance at a straightforward bid for power. Perhaps they have learned the Man's lessons so well they cannot imagine themselves succeeding. This is a far greater tragedy than nasty taunts. Social change creeps because social changers crawl. A collapse of vision and heart, protectionism leaves oppressed groups reliant on their oppressors.

As long-term solutions, Delgado and Stefancic write, "Lawyers and social scientists must be prepared to demonstrate through re-search the harm done by racial insults and pornography and to show how the current law's conception of harm can be reasonably ex-panded to include notions of damaged identity" (pp. B2–B3). Gates (1993) calls this the politics of "recovery." He writes, "At the vital center of the hate speech movement is the seductive vision of the therapeutic state. This vision is presaged in the manifesto [*Words That Wound*] itself: 'Too often victims of hate speech find themselves without the words to articulate what they see, feel and know. In the absence of theory and analysis that give them a diagnosis and a name for the injury they have suffered, they internalize the injury done them and are rendered silent in the face of continuing injury. Criti-cal race theory names the injury and identifies its origins.' . . . Indeed," Gates concludes, "in the Republic of Self-Esteem, we are invited to conceive of the lawsuit as therapy" (p. 46).

The substantial research on words, images, and harm has not shown a causal link between expression and harm of any sort, in-cluding damage to the self-esteem of women (Krafka, 1985). Even the Attorney General's Commission exempted words from its rec-ommendations to restrict sexual images. Author Bob Chatelle, chair of the Political Issues Commmittee of the National Writers Union, is a member of the one minority against whom it is legal and in many places praiseworthy to discriminate, homosexuals. In response to the Delgado and Stefancic article, he wrote (Chatelle, 1993), "I had the impression that 'damaged identity' was already actionable under laws governing libel and slander. But what disturbs me most is the now prevailing 'liberal' notion that speech is so 'dangerous' that it must be carefully monitored and often silenced. . . . As a proud member of a sexual minority, I find insulting, demeaning, and degrading your assumption that I'm in need of Big Brother's special protection. In fact, I even find it damaging to my identity" (p. 7).

In framing their argument, Delgado and Stefancic (1993) noted "the emerging cooperation between two groups of reformers": the "legal scholars and social activists [who] have been seeking ways to combat the harm done to members of minority groups by hateful speech" and "scholars and activists [who] have been focusing on the harm done to women by hard-core pornography" (p. B1). Delgado and Stefancic understand the new coalition as this book does: as a union of image-blamers who would ban wrongful speech rather than risk debating it before the public. "Scholars also need to find ways to demonstrate how 'more speech' . . . is not a viable solution," Delgado and Stefancic write (p. B3), putting their efforts to banishing offensive words rather than address their underlying causes. Jonathan Yardley wrote in *The Washington Post National Weekly* (1993), "It's a lot easier to enact a speech code and then to pretend that problems of discrimination have been solved than it is to do the hard work of actually solving the problems. . . . Evasion and euphemism are now our chosen strategies."

Delgado and Stefancic are certain of which speech is wrongful. Their writing is undisturbed by students and faculty who believe that feminist speech or homosexual rights advocacy are hurtful, but sexist or homophobic slurs not. Many oppose gay and feminist advocacy because of religious beliefs, which are protected by Civil Rights law much as are race, ethnicity, and gender. A Christian fundamentalist may believe homosexuality is an abomination and want to say so on campus out loud. Delgado's legal writing does not make clear whose "protected class" status should prevail: the gay man's (sexual orientation) or the fundamentalist's (religion). Should a university's interest in protecting female equality lead it to ban a speech on women's rightful subservience to men, or should the interest in protecting religion shut down an abortion rights rally that many feel advocates the sin of murder?

In the year the Wisconsin code was ruled unconstitutional, the U.S. District Court in Virginia reviewed a case in which a fraternity was accused of racist humor (*Sigma Chi Fraternity v. George Mason University*, 1991). The court wrote, "A more appropriate response to the activities of the fraternity, and one consistent with the First Amendment, would have been instead to say to those offended by . . . [the] speech that their right to protest that speech by all peaceable means would be as stringently safeguarded . . . as would . . . [the] right to engage in it." The Annenberg Washington Program of Northwestern University brought together a panel of lawyers, law professors, judges, and university administrators that concluded (1990), "most attempts to deal with racist and sexist expression through restrictive and punitive measures are problematic from a First Amendment point of view—they do not address the root causes of the problems of racial prejudice and sexism, and may, in fact, be counterproductive." With some sense of weariness, Henry Louis Gates Jr. (1993) wrote, "The problem about which Lawrence worries, that racist speech 'silences members of those groups who are its targets,' would naturally be addressed not through bureaucratic regulations, but through the sort of deconstruction and critique that will enable victims, according to critical race theory, to 'find their voices.' And here lies another painful irony. All this sounds very much like Justice Brandeis's hoary and much-scorned prescription for redressing harmful speech: 'more speech'" (p. 46).

SENSE AND CENSORSHIP

The "more speech" approach to offensive speech may seem well suited to university campuses but naive outside the university, where individuals or small groups face wealthy, vertically integrated media conglomerates. It is the old problem of trying to publish when one does not own the presses. Yet twenty-five years ago, what began as a small ragtag group of student loudmouths convinced the public and media of the folly of the Vietnam War. At the start of the 1960s, most citizens and members of the press were in favor of the U.S. presence in Southeast Asia; by the end of the '60s most, including mainstream news commentators, were against it. The campaign against smoking, twenty years ago the effort of a small, curious group, has persuaded millions of Americans to quit. More recently, politically inexperienced groups of gay men protested against a dearth of AIDS funding and have grown in half a dozen years into impressive lobbying forces with considerable budgets.

Feminists and civil rights activists made nuisances of themselves till they were heard. No public figure says "nigger" today and few say "girl," not because the words were banned but because blacks and women convinced the country that racism and sexism were wrong. If students utter these words on campus, they have not been convinced. Restricting speech or punishing it hardens their views; debates, rallies, and screaming matches—"more speech"—may be the one chance at persuasion. They do not guarantee victory; one's opponents will fight energetically to see their points prevail. But in the war of words, it is better to lose in open debate than to win by thuggery. In a system of debate, one may try again. In a system of enforced speech, one is vulnerable to force. Even if one wins for a time, the system of force prods rebellion. One will soon find one's mouth under someone else's boot.

In the experiment of open debate, women and minorities aired their ideas, both in the mainstream media and in the alternative publications, galleries, and theaters that they built. Writers, theorists, and artists rode the coattails of a political effort and in turn provided a spin for the politics to go another round. The supposedly quicker solution of silencing "bad" speech gives up the game. Having established the precedent of censorship, there is nothing to stop one's views from being silenced next. Protectionist regulations of speech may offer the immediate boons of retribution, as did smashing "demon rum," but they cast their proponents as people of lesser intellect and strength who need protecting.

Stanford University Law Professor Gerald Gunther grew up in Nazi Germany and was called very unflattering things in school. In

1989 he wrote, "My own experiences have certainly not led me to be insensitive to the myriad pains offensive speech can and often does impose. But the lesson I have drawn from my childhood in Nazi Germany and my happier adult life in this country is the need to walk the sometimes difficult path of denouncing the bigot's hateful ideas with all my power yet at the same time challenging any community's attempt to suppress hateful ideas by force of law" (p. 17).

A decade earlier, the American Civil Liberties Union raised a national controversy with their defense of the American Nazi party's right to march through Skokie, Illinois, the home of many Jewish survivors of the Second World War. Aryeh Neier, then ACLU executive director, wrote about his support for the Nazi's right to march (Neier, 1979), "Because we Jews are uniquely vulnerable, I believe we can win only brief respite from persecution in a society in which encounters are settled by power. As a Jew, therefore, . . . I want restraints which prohibit those in power from interfering with my right to speak, my right to publish, or my right to gather with others who also feel threatened. . . . To defend myself, I must restrain power with freedom, even if the temporary beneficiaries are the enemies of freedom" (pp. 4–5).

The people who own the presses, who speak much and loudly, worked hard for that privilege. They did, or their fathers or grandfathers, but someone put in a good deal of time and effort. Power never cedes. To promote new ideas, one has to persuade people to pay attention. One has not only to think, write, or perform but also set up the structures, political and financial, to help unorthodox voices be heard. It is a double load, it takes its toll and has taken up lifetimes. The advantage of having an uncensored republic is that one gets to make one's bid.

The principle behind freedom of expression is not that it automatically secures what one thinks is good or true, but that it is society's best chance at truth in the long run. Justice William Brennan Jr. wrote in 1989, "The First Amendment does not guarantee that other concepts sacred to our Nation as a whole—such as the principle that discrimination based on race is odious and destructive—will go unquestioned in the marketplace of ideas" (Brennan, 1989).

The nation bats ideas back and forth, advancing and modifying its views. The alternative is to let someone appoint himself king and have his way. In 1947, Winston Churchill told Parliament, "It has been said that democracy is the worst form of government, except all those other forms that have been tried."

Democracy takes time; there is no automatic pilot. "The freedom to differ," wrote Justice Jackson in *West Virginia v. Barnette* (1943), "is not limited to things that do not matter much. That would be the mere shadow of freedom. The test of its substance is the right to differ as to things that touch the heart of the existing order."

BIBLIOGRAPHY

Abel, G. (1989, January 25). Transcript from *Today* (television program).

Abramovitz, M., & Piven, F. (1993, September 2). Scapegoating Women on Welfare. *The New York Times*, p. A23.

Abramson, P., & Hayashi, H. (1984). Pornography in Japan: Cross-Cultural and Theoretical Considerations. In N. Malamuth & E. Donnerstein (Eds.), *Pornography and Sexual Aggression* (p. 173). Orlando, FL: Academic Press.

Adult Literacy in America (1993). National Center for Educational Statistics, Office for Educational Research and Improvement, U.S. Department of Education. Washington, DC: U.S. Government Printing Office.

Ageton, S. (1983). *Sexual Assault among Adolescents*. Lexington, MA: Lexington Books.

Allgeier, E. (1990). *Sexual Interactions* (3rd ed.). Lexington, MA: D. C. Heath.

Allgeier, E. (1991). Interview with the author.

American Booksellers Association, Inc. v. Hudnut, 771 F.2d 323 (7th Cir. 1985); affirmed, 475 U.S. 1001 (1986).

American Civil Liberties Union Arts Censorship Project Newsletter, Spring 1993.

American Civil Liberties Union Arts Censorship Project Newsletter, Summer 1993.

American Family Association Factsheet (1990). *Boycott Lil Champ, A Leading Retailer of Pornography in Florida.* Tupelo, Mississippi.

American Family Association Journal (1991, April 6), p. 6.

American Psychological Association (1993). *Violence and Youth: Psychology's Response. Vol. I: Summary Report of the American Psychological Association Commission on Violence and Youth.* Washington, DC: author.

Anderson, W. (1993, September 12). Reading, Writing and Power. *The New York Times*, p. E19.

Andrews, E. (1990, July 13). Government Seeks to Extend Ban on Broadcast of Offensive Shows. *The New York Times*, p. A1.

Andrews, E. (1993a, June 30). 4 Networks Agree to Offer Warnings of Violence on TV. *The New York Times*, p. A1.

Andrews, E. (1993b, July 1). Mild Slap at TV Violence. *The New York Times*, pp. A1, A14.

The Annenberg Washington Program of Northwestern University. (1990, April 12). *Report of Workshop on Racist and Sexist Speech on College and University Campuses.* Washington, DC.

Arce, R. (1988, October 16). Devil's in a B'klyn Dad; Son, 3, Is Stabbed. *The New York Daily News*.

Associated Press (1989, January 27). Attorney: Bundy Sabotaged Appeal with Confessions.

Associated Press (1991a, March 30). Support for Avant-Garde Film Defended. *New York Newsday*.

Associated Press (1991b, January 14). Rape Attempts Decreasing.

Associated Press (1992, March 21). School Restricts "Snow White."

Attorney General's Commission on Pornography (1986). U.S. Department of Justice. Washington, DC: U.S. Government Printing Office.

Ayres, B. D., Jr. (1993, June 7). Christian Right Splits G.O.P. in South. *The New York Times*, p. A12.

Band Is Held Not Liable in Suicides of Two Fans. (1990, August 25). *The New York Times*, p. A11.

Bandura, A., Ross, D., & Ross, S. (1963). Imitation of Film Mediated Aggressive Models. *Journal of Abnormal and Social Psychology,66*, 3–11.

Barbaree, H., & Marshall, W. (1991). The Role of Male Sexual Arousal in Rape: Six Models. *Journal of Consulting and Clinical Psychology, 59*(5), 621–630.

Baron, L. (1987). Immoral, Inviolate or Inconclusive? *Society, 24*(5), 6–12.

Baron, L. (1990). Pornography and Gender Equality: An Empirical Analysis. *Journal of Sex Research, 27*, 363–380.

Baron, L., & Straus, M. (1984). Sexual Stratification, Pornography, and Rape in the United States. In N. Malamuth & E. Donnerstein (Eds.), *Pornography and Sexual Aggression* (pp. 185–209). Orlando, FL: Academic Press.

Baron, L., & Straus, M. (1985). Legitimate Violence, Pornography, and Sexual Inequality as Explanations for State and Regional Differences in Rape. Unpublished manuscript. Yale University, New Haven, CT.

Baron, L., & Straus, M. (1986). Rape and Its Relation to Social Disorganization, Pornography, and Sexual Inequality in the United States. Unpublished manuscript. Yale University, New Haven, CT.

Baron, L., & Straus, M. (1987). Four Theories of Rape: A Macrosociological Analysis. *Social Problems, 34*(5), 467–489.

Baron, L., & Straus, M. (1989). *Four Theories of Rape in Amerian Society: A State-level Analysis.* New Haven, CT: Yale University Press.

Baron, R. (1974a). The Aggression-Inhibiting Influence of Heightened Sexual Arousal. *Journal of Personality and Social Psychology, 30*(3), 318–322.

Baron, R. (1974b). Sexual Arousal and Physical Aggression: The Inhibiting Influence of "Cheesecake" and Nudes. *Bulletin of the Psychonomic Society, 3,* 337–339.

Baron, R. (1977). *Human Aggression*, New York: Plenum Press.

Baron, R., & Bell, P. (1973). Effects of Heightened Sexual Arousal on Physical Aggression. *Proceedings of the 81st Convention of the American Psychological Association, 8,* 171–172.

Baron, R., & Bell, P. (1977). Sexual Arousal and Aggression by Males: Effects of Type of Erotic Stimuli and Prior Provocation. *Journal of Personality and Social Psychology, 35,* 79–87.

Beck, A., Kline, S., & Greenfeld, L. (1988). Survey of Youth in Custody, 1987. Bureau of Justice Statistics, Special Report. Office of Justice Programs, U.S. Department of Justice. Washington DC: U.S. Government Printing Office.

Becker, J., & Levine, E. (1986). Dissenting Report to Attorney General Edwin Meese's Commission on Pornography. See, Attorney General's Commission on Pornography. U.S. Department of Justice. Washington, DC: U.S. Government Printing Office.

Becker, J., & Stein, R. (1991). Is Sexual Erotica Associated with Sexual Deviance in Adolescent Males? *International Journal of Law and Psychiatry, 14*, 85–95.

Belson, W. (1978). *Television Violence and the Adolescent Boy.* Farmborough, Hants, England: Saxon House, Teakfield.

Berger, J. (1993, July 10). Priest Enters Plea of Guilty to Sex Abuse. *The New York Times*, pp. 21, 24.

Bergin, A., & Lambert, M. (1978). The Evaluation of Therapeutic Outcomes. In S. Garfield & A. Bergin (Eds.), *Handbook of Psychotherapy and Behavior Change: An Empirical Analysis* (2nd ed., pp. 139–190). New York: Wiley.

Berman, M. (1991, January 21). NC-17 X'd Out at Blockbuster; Wildmon, AFA Boycott Lifted. *Variety*.

Bernstein, R. (1993, May 30). Cap, Gown and Gag: The Struggle for Control. *The New York Times*, p. D3.

Berry, J. (1992). *Lead Us Not into Temptation.* New York: Doubleday.

Boylan, A., & Taub, N. (1981). *Adult Domestic Violence: Constitutional, Legislative and Equitable Issues.* Chicago: National Clearinghouse for Legal Services.

Brandenburg v. Ohio, 395 U.S. 444 (1969).

Brannigan, A. (1987). Is Obscenity Criminogenic? *Society, 24*(5), 12–19.

Brennan, W. Jr., *Texas v. Johnson*, 109 S. Ct. 2533, 2545 (1989).

The British Inquiry into Obscenity and Film Censorship (1979), (Williams Committee), London, England: Home Office Research and Planning Unit.

Britton, P. (1993a). Comparative Quantitative Analysis of the Similarities and Differences in Female- Versus Male-Directed/Produced/Written Commercial Sex Films and Videos (1980–1990). Doctoral dissertation, Institute for Advanced Study of Human Sexuality, San Francisco.

Britton, P. (1993b). Interview with the author.

Brody, J. (1990, January 23). Scientists Trace Aberrant Sexuality. *The New York Times,* pp. C1, C12.

Bruno v. McGuire, 4 Family Law Reporter, 3095 (1978).

The Budget Fight Has Just Begun. (1993, August 8). *The New York Times*, p. D14.

Bureau of Justice Statistics (1992). *Criminal Victimization in the United States, 1990.* Washington, DC: U.S. Government Printing Office.

Burgess, A., Hartman, C., MacCausland, M., & Powers, P. (1984). Response Patterns in Children and Adolescents Exploited through Sex Rings and Pornography. *American Journal of Psychiatry, 141*, 656–662.

Burstyn v. Wilson, 343 U.S. 495 (1952).

Burstyn, V. (Ed.). (1985). *Women against Censorship.* Vancouver, British Columbia: Douglas & McIntyre Ltd.

Butterfield, F. (1993, January 31). Studies Find a Family Link to Criminality. *The New York Times*, pp. A1, A16.

cad (1993, June). *Off Our Backs*, p. 4.

Campbell, A. (1993). *Men, Women, and Aggression.* New York: Basic Books.

Campbell, C. (1989, August 22). The Missionary Position: The Devil Is a Reverend. *The Village Voice*, p. 35.

Cannon, C. (1987, December 30–31). *San Jose Mercury News.*

Carter, B. (1993, June 22). Police Drama under Fire for Sex and Violence. *The New York Times*, p. C13.

Celis, W., III. (1993, September 9). Study Says Half of Adults in U.S. Lack Reading and Math Abilities. *The New York Times*, pp. A1, A22.

Centerwall, B. (1993). Television and Violent Crime. *The Public Interest, 111*, 56–71.

Chaffee, S., Gerbner, G., Hamburg, B., Pierce, C., Rubinstein, E., Siegel, A., & Singer, J. (1984). Defending the Indefensible. *Society, 21*(6), 30-35.

Charren, P. (1993, July 7). It's 8 P.M. Where Are Your Parents? *The New York Times*, pp. A14–15.

Charting the Adult Industry (1991). Buyer's Guide, *Adult Video News,* 6(2), pp. 26–28.

Charting the Adult Industry (1992). Adult Entertainment Guide, *Adult Video News*, pp. 27–28.

Charting the Adult Industry (1993). Adult Entertainment Guide, *Adult Video News*, pp. 26–28.

Chatelle, B. (1993). "Liberals" v. The First Amendment. *Political Issues Committee Newsletter, II*(1), 7.

Check, J. V. P. (1984). The Effects of Violent and Nonviolent Pornography. Report to the Department of Justice, Ottawa, Ontario, Canada: Department of Justice, Department of Supply and Services contract 05SV, (1920) 0-3-0899.

Check, J., & Malamuth, N. (1984). Can There Be Positive Effects of Participation in Pornography Experiments? *Journal of Sex Research, 20*, 14–31.

Chilman, C. (1983). *Adolescent Sexuality in a Changing American Society*. New York: Wiley.

Chodorow, N. (1978). *The Reproduction of Mothering: Psychoanalysis and the Sociology of Gender*. Los Angeles: University of California Press.

Christensen, F. (1993). Does Use of Pornography Lead to Violence? *Handbook of Human Sexuality, 8.*

Cline, V. (1970). How Violence Affects Children. *Life, 68*, pp. 57–58.

Cline, V. (1973). Desensitization of Children to Television Violence. *Journal of Personality and Social Psychology, 27*, 360.

Cline, V. (Ed.). (1974). *Where Do You Draw the Line? Explorations in Media Violence, Pornography and Censorship*. Provo, Utah: Brigham Young University Press.

Cline, V. (1975). TV Violence: How It Damages Your Children. *Ladies Home' Journal, 92*, p. 75.

Coliver, S. (Ed.). (1992). *Striking a Balance: Hate Speech, Freedom of Expression and Non-discrimination*. Contributing editors Kevin Boyle and Frances D'Souza. Article 19, International Centre Against Censorship. London and Human Rights Centre. University of Essex.

Comstock, R., & Paik, H. (1990). The Effects of Television Violence on Aggressive Behavior: A Meta-analysis. Washington, DC: Unpublished report to the National Academy of Sciences Panel on the Understanding and Control of Violent Behavior.

Conable, G. (1991, November 16; 1993, August 25). Personal communications.

Condron, M., & Nutter, D. (1988). A Preliminary Examination of the Pornography Experience of Sex Offenders, Paraphiliacs, Sexual Dysfunction Patients, and Controls Based on Meese Commission Recommendations. *Journal of Sex and Marital Therapy, 14*(4), 285–298.

Cook, F., Tyler, T., Goetz, E., Gordon, M., Protess, D., Leff, D., & Molotch, H. (1983). Media and Agenda Setting: Effects on the Public, Interest Group Leaders, Policy Makers, and Policy. *Public Opinion Quarterly, 47*, 16–35.

Cooke, P. (1993, August 14). TV Causes Violence? Says Who? *The New York Times*, p. A19.

Cox News Service (1990). Showing Slasher Films Reduces Fights in Prison.

Davies, P., & Neve, B. (Eds.). (1981). *Cinema, Politics and Society in America*. New York: St. Martin's Press.

De Crow, K. (1993, June 30). Missing the Point. *Syracuse New Times*.

De Grazia, E., & Newman, R. (1982). *Banned Films: Movies, Censors and the First Amendment*. New York: R. R. Bowker.

De Grazia, E. (1992). *Girls Lean Back Everywhere: The Law of Obscenity and the Assault on Genius*. New York: Random House.

Delgado, R., & Stefancic, J. (1993, August). Overcoming Legal Barriers to Regulating Hate Speech on Campus. *Chronicle of Higher Education*, pp. B1–B3.

D'Emilio, J., & Freedman, E. (1988). *Intimate Matters: A History of Sexuality in America*. New York, Harper & Row.

DeVito, D. (1987, November). Personal communication.

Dinnerstein, D. (1976). *The Maid and the Minotaur: Sexual Arrangements and Human Malaise*. New York: Harper & Row.

Donnerstein, E. (1983). Erotica and Human Aggression. In R. Green and E. Donnerstein (Eds.), *Aggression: Theoretical and Empirical Reviews* (pp.). New York: Academic Press.

Donnerstein, E. (1984). Pornography: Its Effect on Violence against Women. In N. Malamuth & E. Donnerstein (Eds.), *Pornography and Sexual Aggression* (pp.). Orlando, FL: Academic Press.

Donnerstein, E. (1986). Techniques Designed to Mitigate the Impact of Mass Media Sexual Violence on Adolescents and Adults. Paper presented to Surgeon General's Workshop on Pornography. Report of the Surgeon General's Workshop on Pornography and Public Health, 1986.

Donnerstein, E., & Berkowitz, L. (1981). Victim Reactions in Aggressive-Erotic Films as a Factor in Violence against Women. *Journal of Personality and Social Psychology, 41*, 710–724.

Donnerstein, E., & Linz, D. (1986, December). The Question of Pornography. *Psychology Today*, pp. 56–59.

Donnerstein, E., & Linz, D. (1990). Evidence on the Causal Connection between Exposure to Penthouse Magazine and Anti-social Conduct. Prepared for Helen K. Wild, Simpson, Grierson, Butler and White, Aukland, New Zealand.

Donnerstein, E., Linz, D., & Penrod, S. (1987). *The Question of Pornography: Research Findings and Policy Implications*. New York: Free Press.

Doob, L. (1961). *Communication in Africa*. New Haven, CT: Yale University Press.

Douglas, J. (1993). Personal communication.

Dreifus, C. (1992, September 5). TV's Watchdog from Tupelo. *TV Guide*, pp. 11–17.

Duggan, L. (1984, October 16). Censorship in the Name of Feminism. *The Village Voice*, pp. 11, 12, 16, 17, 42.

Dworkin, A. (1974). *Woman Hating*. New York: Dutton.

Dworkin, A. (1981). *Pornography: Men Possessing Women*. New York: Perigee Press.

Dworkin, A. (1987). *Intercourse*. New York: Free Press.

Elson, J. (1992, March 30). Passions over Pornography. *Time*, p. 53.

Eron, L. (1982). Parent-Child Interaction, Television Violence, and Aggression of Children. *American Psychologist, 37*, 197–211.

Eron, L. (1986). Interventions to Mitigate the Psychosocial Effects of Media Violence on Aggressive Behavior. *Journal of Social Science, 42*, 155–169.

Eron, L., & Huesmann, L. (1980). Adolescent Aggression and Television. *Annals of the New York Academy of Sciences, 347*, 319–331.

Eron, L., & Huesmann, L. (1984). The Relation of Prosocial Behavior to the Development of Aggression and Psychopathology. *Aggressive Behavior, 10*, 201–212.

Eron, L., & Huesmann, L. (1987). The Stability of Aggressive Behavior in Cross-National Comparisons. In C. Kagitcibasi (Ed.), *Growth and Progress in Cross-Cultural Psychology* (pp. 207–218). Lisse, Holland: Swets and Zeitlinger.

Eron, L., & Huesmann, L. (1990). The Stability of Aggressive Behavior— Even Unto the Third Generation. In M. Lewis and S. Miller (Eds.), *Handbook of Developmental Psychopathology* (pp. 147–156). New York: Plenum Press.

Eysenck, H. (1978). Psychology and Obscenity: A Factual Look at Some of the Problems. In R. Dhavan and C. Davies (Eds.), *Censorship and Obscenity* (pp. 148–182). London: Martin Robertson.

Fabes, R., & Strouse, J. (1987). Perceptions of Responsible and Irresponsible Models of Sexuality: A Correlational Study. *Journal of Sex Research, 23*, 70–84.

FACT. Feminist Anti Censorship Taskforce brief of *amici curiae* in *American Booksellers Association, Inc., et al. v. William Hudnut III, et al.* 771 F2d 323 (7th Circuit) (1985). Nan Hunter and Sylvia Law, attorneys of record.

Farber, M. (1990, August 3). Covenant Report Is Said to Find Sex Misconduct. *The New York Times*, pp. A1, B4.

Feldman, W., Feldman, E., Goodman, J., McGrath, P., Pless, R., Corsini,

L., & Bennett, S. (1991). Is Child Sexual Abuse Really Increasing in Prevalence? An Analysis of the Evidence. *Pediatrics, 88*(1), 29–33.

Feminist Bookstore News (1993, March/April).

Feminists for Free Expression (1992a, February 14). New York: Letter to the Senate Judiciary Committee.

Feminists for Free Expression (1992b). Brief of *amicus curiae* in *Ferris Alexander Sr. v. United States of America.*, ____ U.S. ____, 113 S. Ct. 26766 (1993). Helen Mickiewicz, attorney of record.

Feminists for Free Expression. Brief of *amicus curiae* in *Theresa Harris v. Forklift Systems, Inc.*, Supreme Court No. 92-1168 (1993). Cathy Crosson, attorney of record.

Ferraro, T. (1986, November 23). Playboy Redux, and Christie Hefner. United Press International.

Feshback, S., & Singer, R. (1971). *Television and Aggression: An Experimental Field Study.* San Francisco: Jossey-Bass.

Figlio, R. (1986a). Letter to Dr. Sophia Fotopoulos at American University, School of Education, Washington, DC. In, Vol. 1: *Overview of the Project, "A Content Analysis of Playboy, Penthouse and Hustler Magazines with Special Attention to the Portrayal of Children, Crime and Violence."* Washington, DC.

Finan, C., & Castro, A. (1992). *The Rev. Donald E. Wildmon's Crusade for Censorship, 1977–1992.* New York: Media Coalition.

Fisher, W., & Byrne, D. (1978). Sex Differences in Response to Erotica? Love Versus Lust. *Journal of Personality and Social Psychology, 36,* 117–125.

Fleishman, S. (1972, March 15). Chasing our Unconscious Scapegoats. *Psychiatric News.*

Freedman, J. (1984). Effects of Television Violence on Aggressiveness. *Psychological Bulletin, 96,* 227–246.

Freedman, J. (1986). Television Violence and Aggression: The Debate Continues. *Psychological Bulletin, 100,* 364–371.

French, T. (1993, August 22). Parents Are the Real Dropouts. *The New York Times*, The Week in Review, p. 15.

Gardner, G. (1987). *The Censorship Papers: Movie Censorship Letters from the Hays Office, 1934 to 1968.* New York: Dodd, Mead.

Gates, H. Jr. (1993, September 20 and 27). Let Them Talk: Why Civil Liberties Pose No Threat to Civil Rights. *The New Republic*, pp. 37–49.

Gay, V. (1991, March 18). Group Targets 'Absolute Strangers.' *New York Newsday*, pp. 53, 57.

Gaylor, A. (1988). *Betrayal of Trust.* Madison, WI: Freethought Today.

Gebhard, P., Gagnon, J., Pomeroy, W., & Christenson, C. (1965). *Sex Offenders: An Analysis of Types*. New York: Harper & Row.

Gentry, C. (1991). Pornography and Rape: An Empirical Analysis. *Deviant Behavior: An Interdisciplinary Journal, 12*, 277–288.

Giarretto, H. (1991, April). Statement from the Child Sexual Abuse Treatment Program: Statistics and Observations.

Gibb, C. (1992, May). Project P Targets Lesbian Porn. *Quota Magazine*.

Gillan, P. (1978). Therapeutic Uses of Obscenity. In R. Dhavan and C. Davies (Eds.), *Censorship and Obscenity* (pp. 127–147). London: Martin Robertson.

Ginsberg v. New York, 390 U.S. 629 (1968).

Goldman, R., & Goldman, J. (1982). *Children's Sexual Thinking*. London: Routledge & Kegan Paul.

Goldstein, M., & Kant, H. (1973). *Pornography and Sexual Deviance*. A Report of the Legal and Behavioral Institute. Berkeley: University of California Press.

Goldstein, M., Kant, H., Judd, L., Rice, C., & Green, R. (1970). Exposure to Pornography and Sexual Behavior in Deviant and Normal Groups. Technical Reports of the Commission on Obscenity and Pornography, Vol. 7, Washington, DC: U.S. Government Printing Office.

Goleman, D. (1986, May 17). Researchers Dispute Pornography Report on Its Use of Data. *The New York Times*, p. A1.

Goleman, D. (1991a, December 10). New Studies Map the Mind of the Rapist. *The New York Times*, pp. C1, C10.

Goleman, D. (1991b, May 7). New View of Fantasy: Much Is Found Perverse. *The New York Times*, pp. B5, B7.

Goleman, D. (1993, August 11). Hope Seen for Curbing Youth Violence. *The New York Times*, p. A10.

Goody, J. (1977). *The Domestication of the Savage Mind*. New York: Cambridge University Press.

Gottlieb (1990, January 7). Banning Bigoted Speech: Stanford Weighs Rules. *San Jose Mercury-News*, p. 3.

Graham-Yooll, A. (Ed.). (1992). *Index on Censorship, 3*, 40.

Granberry, M. (1993, May 12). A Wave of Censorship Hits the U.S. *The Sacramento Bee Final*, pp. 1, 6.

Greenberg, B., Linsangan, R., Soderman, A., Heeter, C. (1988). Adolescents and Their Reactions to Television Sex. Report #5, Project CAST.

Greenhouse, L. (1992, June 23). High Court Voids Law Singling Out Crimes of Hatred. *The New York Times*, pp. A1, A17.

Grogg, S. (1989). Personal communication.

Gunther, G. (1989, March 15). *Standford University Campus Report*, p. 17.

Harlow, C. (1991, January).Female Victims of Violent Crime. NCJ-126826. Bureau of Justice Statistics, Office of Justice Programs. Washington, DC: U.S. Department of Justice.

Haroian, L. (1988). Interview, Society for the Scientific Study of Sex.

Hartigan, P. (1993, April 3). Clinton Gives Mixed Signals on the Arts. *The Boston Globe*, Living Section, p. 23.

Heffner, R. (1989, March). Personal communication.

Heins, M. (1993a). *Sex, Sin, and Blasphemy.* New York: The New Press.

Heins, M. (1993b). Portrait of a Much Abused Lady. *Index on Censorship, 22(1)*, 9–10.

Henderson, A. (1987). *The Evidence Continues to Grow: Parent Involvement Improves Student Achievement.* Columbia, MD: National Coalition of Citizens in Education.

Hentoff, N. (1992, April 4). Pornography War Among Feminists. *The Washington Post*, p. A23.

Herbert, B. (1993a, August 15). Violence and the Young. *The New York Times*, section 4, p. 15.

Herbert, B. (1993b, August 11). Killing 'Just for Whatever.' *The New York Times*, p. A15.

Herbert, B. (1993c, July 11). Violence in Real Life. *The New York Times*, p. A19.

Her Majesty the Queen against Fringe Product, Inc. and 497906 Ontario Limited. (1989, November 21). Court File No. 4079. Ottawa, Ontario, Canada.

Herrman, M., & Bordner, D. (1983). Attitudes toward Pornography in a Southern Community. *Criminology, 21*, 349–374.

Honan, W. (1989, November 9). Arts Endowment Withdraws Grant for AIDS Show. *The New York Times*, pp. A1, C28.

Honan, W. (1991, February 21). Arts Agency Voids Pledge on Obscenity, *The New York Times*, p. C14.

Howard, W., & Lane, K. (1984a, January 31). Porno Studies Funded by Regnery Probed by House Panel as 'Waste' of Tax Dollars. *Child Protection Report*, p. 1.

Howard, W., & Lane, K. (1984b, January 31). 'Flimsy' Credentials Questioned. *Child Protection Report*, p. 2.

Howitt, D., & Cumberbatch, G. (1990). *Pornography: Impacts and Influences. A Review of Available Research Evidence on the Effects of Pornography.* London, England: Home Office Research and Planning Unit.

Huesmann, L. (1982). Television Violence and Aggressive Behavior. In D. Pearl, L. Bouthilet, & J. Lazar (Eds.), *Television and Behavior: Ten Years of Scientific Progress and Implications for the Eighties: Vol 2. Technical Reviews* (pp. 126–137). Washington, DC: U.S. Government Printing Office.

Huesmann, L., Eron, L., Lefkowitz, M., & Walder, L. (1984). Stability of Aggression over Time and Generations. *Developmental Psychology, 20*, 1120–1134.

Huesmann, L., Eron, L., & Yarmel, P. (1987). Intellectual Functioning and Aggression. *Journal of Personality and Social Psychology, 52*(1), 232–240.

Huesmann, L., Lagerspetz, K., & Eron, L. (1984). Intervening Variables in the TV Violence–Aggression Relation: Evidence from Two Countries. *Developmental Psychology, 20*, 746–775.

Huizinga, J. (1950). *Homo Ludens: A Study of the Play Element in Culture*. Boston: Beacon Press.

Hyde, J. (1989). *Understanding Human Sexuality*. New York: McGraw-Hill.

Indecent Publications Tribunal Decision. (1990, November 20, 21, 27). P. J. Cartwright, chair. Wellington, New Zealand.

Intons-Peterson, M., & Roskos-Ewoldsen, B. (1989). Mitigating the Effects of Violent Pornography. In S. Gubar and J. Hoff (Eds.), *For Adult Users Only: The Dilemma of Violent Pornography* (pp. 218–239). Bloomington: Indiana University Press.

Intons-Peterson, M., Roskos-Ewoldsen, B., Thomas, L., Shirely, M., & Blut, D. (1987). Will Educational Materials Offset Negative Effects of Violent Pornography? Unpublished manuscript. Indiana University, Bloomington, IN.

Jordan, M. (1992, September 2). Reports of School Censorship Increase: Survey Finds 50 Percent Jump; Religious Views Prompt Many Cases. *The Washington Post*, p. A19.

Jowett, G. (1976). *Film: The Democratic Art*. Boston: Little, Brown.

Kalikow, P. (1991). Personal communication.

Kallen, H. (1930). *Indecency and the Seven Arts*. New York: H. Liveright.

Kendrick, W. (1987). *The Secret Museum*. New York: Viking Press.

Kendrick, W. (1991). *The Thrill of Fear: 250 Years of Scary Entertainment*. New York: Grove Press.

Kilian, M. (1990, April 22). *The Chicago Tribune*, Tempo Section, p. 5.

Klawans, S. (1994, February 25). Personal communication.

Klein, M. (1992, April 11). Censorship and Fear of Sexuality. Paper to the Scientific Study of Sex Conference, Eastern Region Convention.

Koltko, M. (1993, August 18). Personal correspondence.

Kozinn, A. (1990, July 2). Nude Characters to Remain in City Opera Production. *The New York Times,* p. A14.

Kracauer, S. (1960). *Theory of Film: The Redemption of Physical Reality.* New York: Oxford University Press.

Krafka, C. (1985). Sexually Explicit, Sexually Violent, and Violent Media: Effects of Multiple Naturalistic Exposures and Debriefing on Female Viewers. Doctoral dissertation, University of Wisconsin, Madison, WI.

Kristof, N. (1991, January 15). Law and Order in China Means More Executions. *The New York Times,* p. A2.

Kurtz, H. (1986, November 19). 'Serious Flaws' Shelve $734,371 Study. *The Washington Post,* p. A17.

Kutchinsky, B. (1970). Toward an Explanation of the Decrease in Registered Sex Crimes in Copenhagen. In U.S. Commission on Obscenity and Pornography, Technical Report, Vol. 8.

Kutchinsky, B. (1976). Deviance and Criminality: The Case of a Voyeur in a Peeper's Paradise. *Diseases of the Nervous System, 37(3),* 145–151.

Kutchinsky, B. (1984). Personal correspondence.

Kutchinsky, B. (1985). Pornography and Its Effects in Denmark and the United States: A Rejoinder and Beyond. In *Comparative Social Research: An Annual(8),* 301–330.

Kutchinsky, B. (1987). Deception and Propaganda. *Society, 24(5),* 21–24.

Kutchinsky, B. (1991). Pornography and Rape: Theory and Practice? Evidence from Crime Data In Four Countries Where Pornography Is Easily Available. *International Journal of Law and Psychiatry,* 14(1&2), 47–64.

Lanning, K. (1992). *Child Molesters: A Behavioral Analysis.* Washington, DC: Behavioral Sciences Unit. FBI.

Lanning, K. (1993, August 18). Interview with the author.

Leonard, K., & Taylor, S. (1983). Exposure to Pornography, Permissive and Non-Permissive Cues, and Male Aggression Towards Females. *Motivation and Emotion, 7(3),* 291–299.

Levy, L. (1993). *Blasphemy: Verbal Offense Against the Sacred.* New York: Knopf.

Lewin, T. (1992a, November 13). Furor on Exhibit at Law School Splits Feminists. *The New York Times,* p. B16.

Lewin, T. (1992b, February 28). Canada Court Says Pornography Harms Women. *The New York Times,* p. B7.

Lewin, T. (1992c, May 10). Feminists Wonder If It Was Progress to Become 'Victims.' *The New York Times*, p. D6.

Lewis, J. (1982). Technology, Enterprise, and American Economic Growth. *Science, 215*, 1204–1211.

Lincoln, Abraham. (1859, April 6). Letter to H. L. Pierce and others.

Linz, D. (1985). Sexual Violence in the Media: Effects on Male Viewers and Implications for Society. Doctoral dissertation, University of Wisconsin, Madison, WI.

Linz, D. (1989). Exposure to Sexually Explicit Materials and Attitudes Toward Rape: A Comparison of Study Results. *Journal of Sex Research, 26*, 50–84.

Linz, D., Donnerstein, E., Land, K., McCall, P., Scott, J., Shafer, B., Klein, L., & Lance, L. (1991). Estimating Community Standards: The Use of Social Science Evidence in an Obscenity Prosecution. *Public Opinion Quarterly, 55*, 80–112.

Linz, D., Donnerstein, E., & Penrod, S. (1984). The Effects of Multiple Exposure to Filmed Violence against Women. *Journal of Communication, 34*, 130–147.

Linz, D., Donnerstein, E., & Penrod, S. (1987). The Findings and Recommendations of the Attorney General's Commission on Pornography: Do the Psychological "Facts" Fit the Political Fury? *American Psychologist, 42*,(10), 946–953.

Linz, D., Donnerstein, E., & Penrod, S. (1988). The Effects of Long-Term Exposure to Violent and Sexually Degrading Depictions of Women. *Journal of Personality and Social Psychology, 55*, 758–768.

Linz, D., Donnerstein, E., Shafer, B., Klein, L., Land, K., McCall, P., Scott, J., & Graesser, A. (in press). Defining the Limits of Public Tolerance for Sexually Explicit and Sexually Violent Materials: A Field Experiment. *Law in Society Review*.

Linz, D., Wilson, B., & Donnerstein, E. (1992). Sexual Violence in the Mass Media: Legal Solutions, Warnings, and Mitigation through Education. *Journal of Social Issues, 48*(1), 145–171.

Louis Harris and Associates (1986). *American Teens Speak: Sex, Myth, TV, and Birth Control*. New York: Planned Parenthood Federation of America.

Louis Harris and Associates (1993). The Annual Metropolitan Life Survey of the American Teacher. New York.

Lyall, S. (1993, December 3). Canada's Morals Police: Serious Books at Risk? *The New York Times*, p. A8.

Lynn, B. (1986). "Civil Rights" Ordinances and the Attorney General's

Commission: New Developments in Pornography Regulation. *Harvard Civil Rights—Civil Liberties Law Review, 21*, 25–125.

Lynn, B. (1993, June). *The Religious Right Is on the March Again.* Silver Spring, MD: Americans United for Separation of Church and State.

MacKinnon, C. (1979). *Sexual Harassment of Working Women.* Hartford, CT: Yale University Press.

MacKinnon, C. (1987). *Feminism Unmodified.* Cambridge, MA: Harvard University Press.

MacKinnon, C. (1993). *Only Words.* Cambridge, MA: Harvard University Press.

MacNeil, Lehrer. (1986, July 9). Taking Aim at Porn. Transcript #2813.

Malamuth, N. (1978a). Erotica, Aggression and Perceived Appropriateness. The 86th convention of the American Psychological Association, Toronto, Ontario, Canada.

Malamuth, N. (1978b). The Sexual Responsiveness of College Students to Rape Depictions: Inhibitory and Disinhibitory Effects. *Journal of Personality and Social Psychology, 14*, 121–137.

Malamuth, N., & Ceniti, J. (1986). Repeated Exposure to Violent and Nonviolent Pornography: Likelihood of Raping Ratings and Laboratory Aggression Against Women. *Aggressive Behavior, 12*, 129–137.

Malamuth, N., & Check, J. (1984). Debriefing Effectiveness Following Exposure to Pornographic Rape Depictions. *Journal of Sex Research, 20*, 1–13.

Mancini, J., & Mancini, S. (1983). The Family's Role in Sex Education: Implications for Educators. *Journal of Sex Education and Therapy, 9*, 16–21.

Margolick, D. (1993, December 22). Sex Abuse Cases Threaten to Bankrupt an Archdiocese. *The New York Times,* pp. A1, A21.

Markels, G. (1990, November 26). Ratings Board Conference. Los Angeles/New York: Motion Picture Association of America.

Marriott, N. (1993, August 15). Hard-Core Rap Lyrics Stir Black Backlash. *The New York Times*, pp. 1, 42.

Mathews, J. (1987, June 1). Change in Film Ratings Favored: Parents Want More Details: Producers Want Status Quo. *The Los Angeles Times*, p. 9.

McCaslin, J. (1986, March 27). Official Says $734,371 to Peer at Porn Was Wasteful. *The Washington Times.*

McCormack, T. (1993, May 8). Paper to *Sex Panic: Women, Censorship and Pornography.* Symposium conducted by The National Coalition Against Censorship, New York.

McGuire, W. (1985). Attitudes and Attitude Change. In G. Lindzey & E.

Aronson (Eds.), *Handbook of Social Psychology* (3rd ed., pp.). New York: Random House.

McGuire, W. (1986). The Myth of Massive Media Impact: Savagings and Salvagings. In *Public Communication and Behavior*, (pp. 173–255). Orlando, FL: Academic Press.

McKay, H., & Dolff, D. (1984). Working Papers on Pornography and Prostitution. Report #13. The Impact of Pornography: An Analysis of Research and Summary of Findings. Policy Programs and Research Branch, Research and Statistics Section. Ottawa, Ontario, Canada: Department of Justice.

McLeod, J., Atkin, C., & Chaffee, S. (1972). Adolescents, Parents and Television Use: Adolescent Self-Report Measures from Maryland and Wisconsin Samples. In G. Comstock & E. Rubinstein (Eds.), *Television and Social Behavior: Vol. 3. Television and Adolescent Aggressiveness* (pp. 177–238). Washington DC: U.S. Government Printing Office.

Milavsky, J., Kessler, R., Stipp, H., & Rubens, W. (1982). *Television and Aggression: Results of a Panel Study*. New York: Academic Press.

Minzey, D. (1991, April 12). Personal communication.

Mitchell, J. (1990, November 19). National Drive to Establish Local Film and Video Ratings Boards. Los Angeles/New York: Motion Picture Association of America.

Money, J. (1984a). Paraphilias: Phenomenology and Classification. *American Journal of Psychotherapy, 38*(2), 164–179.

Money, J. (1984b). *Oversight on Pornography Magazines of a Variety of Courses, Inquiring into the Subject of Their Impact on Child Abuse, Child Molestation, and Problems of Conduct against Women: Hearings before the Subcommittee on Juvenile Justice of the Committee of the Judiciary*, 98th Congress, 324 at 342.

Money, J., & Lamacz, M. (1989). *Vandalized Lovemaps*. New York: Prometheus Books.

Morris, M. (1985). Governmental Regulation of Pornography: Rhetoric of Harm. Paper to the American Sociological Association.

Mosher, D. (1989). Threat to Sexual Freedom: Moralistic Intolerance Instills a Spiral of Silence. *Journal of Sex Research, 26*, 492–409.

Mydans, S. (1993, November 30). 11 Friars Molested Seminary Students, Church Inquiry Says. *The New York Times*, pp. A1, B8.

A Move to Protect Women from 'Street Harassment.' (1993, July 2). *The New York Times*, p. D19.

National Advisory Council on Economic Opportunity. (1981). *Final Report:*

The American Promise: Equal Justice and Economic Opportunity. Washington, DC: U.S. Government Printing Office.

National Campaign for Freedom of Expression (1993, March). NEA Four Update: Government Appeals Decency Ruling.

National Coalition on Television Violence. (1988, March 14). Study Finds Violent Trend in Bestselling Fiction: Experts Call Trend Unhealthy. New York: Champaign, Illinois.

National Institutes of Mental Health (1982). *Television and Behavior: Ten years of Scientific Progress and Implications for the Eighties. Vol. 1. Summary Report.* Washington, DC: U.S. Government Printing Office.

National Research Council (1993). *Understanding and Preventing Violence.* Washington, DC: National Academy Press.

Neier, A. (1979). *Defending My Enemy: American Nazis, The Skokie Case and the Risks of Freedom.* New York: American Civil Liberties Union.

Nieto, S. (1992). *Affirming Diversity: The Sociopolitical Context of Multicultural Education.* New York: Longman.

Nobile, P. (1989a). Personal correspondence.

Nobile, P. (1989b, June). The Making of a Monster. *Playboy*, pp. 41–45.

Noelle-Neumann, E. (1974). Spiral of Silence: A Theory of Public Opinion. *Journal of Communication 24*, 43–51.

Noelle-Neumann, E. (1984). *The Spiral of Silence: Public Opinion—Our Social Skin.* Chicago: University of Chicago Press.

O'Connor, J. (1993, July 11). Labeling Prime-Time Violence Is Still a Band-Aid Solution. *The New York Times*, C1, C26.

Olmstead v. United States, 277 U.S. 438, 478 (1928).

Padgett, V., Brislin-Slutz, J., & Neal, J. (1989). Pornography, Erotica and Negative Attitudes Towards Women: The Effects of Repeated Exposure. *Journal of Sex Research, 26*, 479–491.

Paige, E., McCullaugh, J., & Sweeting, P. (1991, January 26). Blockbuster Says It Won't Carry 'NC-17' Videos. *Billboard*, p. 1, 105.

Pally, M. (1985a, June 29). Ban Sexism Not Pornography. *The Nation*, pp. 794–797.

Pally, M. (1985b, October 5). Putting an End to Violence Against Women: What Will Do the Job? Paper presented to the Harvard–MIT Colloquium on Pornography, Cambridge, MA.

Pally, M. (1990, September) Cincinnati: City Under Siege. *Penthouse*, pp. 149–153, 202, 211.

Palys, T. (1986). Testing the Common Wisdom: The Social Content of Video Pornography. *Canadian Psychology, 27*, pp. 22–35.

Panek, R. (1990, March 21). Nightmare on Hillside Avenue. *7 Days*, pp. 20–24.

Parachini, A. (1990, April 20). Survey Finds Wide Support for Bush's Stance on NEA. Opinion: Survey Also Found That 93% of Americans Believe Public Has the Right to View Controversial Artworks. *The Los Angeles Times*, p. 12.

Pareles, J. (1991, June 2). Sex, Lies and the Trouble with Videotapes. *The New York Times*, pp. C31, C40.

Parke, R., Berkowitz, L., Leyens, J., West S., & Sebastian, R. (1977). Some Effects of Violent and Nonviolent Movies on the Behavior of Juvenile Delinquents. In L. Berkowitz (Ed.), *Advances in Experimental Social Psychology (Vol. 10)* (pp. 135–172). New York: Academic Press.

Pattison, R. (1982). *On Literacy: The Politics of the Word from Homer to the Age of Rock*. New York: Oxford University Press.

Peterson, J. (1988, October). The Big Lie: Reisman Revisited. *Playboy*, pp. 45–52.

Peterson, J., Moore, K., & Furstenburg, F. (1984). Television Viewing and Early Initiation of Sexual Intercourse: Is There a Link? Paper to the American Psychological Association.

Peterson, J. (1987, August). Praise the Lord and Pass the Popcorn. *Playboy*, p. 41.

Pope, Darrell. (1977). Masters thesis, Michigan State University, East Lansing, MI.

Presbyterians Adopt Guidelines to Curb Sex Misconduct by Clergy (1991, June 12). *The New York Times*, p. A20.

Prioleau, L., Murdock, M., & Brody, N. (1983). An Analysis of Psychotherapy versus Placebo Studies. *The Behavioral and Brain Sciences, 6*, 275–310.

The Progressive (1992, May). No Comment, p. 11.

Quindlen, A. (1990, September 20) Suicide Solution. *The New York Times*, p. A21.

Reiss, A., Jr., & Roth, J. (Eds.). (1993). *Understanding and Preventing Violence*. Washington, DC: National Academy Press.

Ressler, R., Burgess, A., & Douglas, J. (1988). *Sexual Homicide: Patterns and Motives*. Lexington, MA: D. C. Heath.

Rohde, S. (1991, December). Campus Speech Codes: Politically Correct, Constitutionally Wrong. *Los Angeles Lawyer*, pp. 23–25, 44–51.

Roiphe, K. (1993a, June 13). Date Rape's Other Victim. *The New York Times Magazine*, pp. 26, 28, 30, 40, 68.

Roiphe, K. (1993b). *The Morning After: Sex, Fear and Feminism on Campus*. Boston: Little, Brown.

Roland, W. Jr. (1983). *Policy Uses of Communication Research*. Beverly Hills, CA: Sage.

Rosenbaum, J., & Prinsky, L. (1987a). 'Leer-ics' or Lyrics: Teenage Impressions of Rock and Roll. *Youth and Society, 18*, 385–397.

Rosenbaum, J., & Prinsky, L. (1987b). Sex, Violence and Rock 'n' Roll. *Popular Music and Society, 11*, 79–90.

Rosier, L. (1993, September 14). Let's Talk about Sex. *The Village Voice*, pp. 29–35.

Royalle, C. (1987). Personal communication.

Rust v. Sullivan, 500 U.S. 173 (1991).

Saffron, I. (1989, June 4). Fugitive Was at War with Family He Killed 18 Years Ago, Police Say. *Chicago Tribune*, section 1, p. 31.

Sante, L. (1991). *Low Life: Lures and Snares of Old New York*. New York: Farrar, Straus and Giroux.

Schauer, F. (1987). Causation Theory and the Causes of Sexual Violence. *American Bar Foundation Research Journal*, Fall (4), pp. 737–770.

Schechter, S. (1982). *Women and Male Violence: The Visions and Struggles of the Battered Women's Movement*. Boston: South End Press.

Scheinfeld, L. (1986, May–June). Ratings: The Big Chill. *Film Comment*, pp. 9–13.

Scott, J. (1985, May 26–31). Violence and Erotic Material—The Relationship between Adult Entertainment and Rape. The American Association for the Advancement of Science Annual Meeting. Los Angeles.

Scott, J., & Cuvelier, S. (1987a). Sexual Violence in Playboy Magazine: A Longitudinal Content Analysis. *Journal of Sex Research, 23*(4), pp. 534–539.

Scott, J., & Cuvelier, S. (1987b). Violence in *Playboy* Magazine: A Longitudinal Analysis. *Archives of Sexual Behavior, 16*(4), pp. 279–288.

Scott, J., & Schwalm, L. (1988a). Pornography and Rape: An Examination of Adult Theater Rates and Rape Rates by State. In J. E. Scott & T. Hirschi (Eds.). *Controversial Issues in Crime and Justice*. Beverly Hills, CA: Sage.

Scott, J., & Schwalm, L. (1988b). Rape Rates and the Circulation Rates of Adult Magazines. *Journal of Sex Research, 24*, 241–250.

Scribner, S., & Cole, M. (1981). *The Psychology of Literacy*. Cambridge, MA: Harvard University Press.

Segal, L. (1990). *Slow Motion: Changing Masculinities Changing Men*. New Brunswick, New Jersey: Rutgers University Press.

Sex Issue. (1981). *Heresies, 3*,(4), issue 12.

Shore, D. (1986, May 16). Personal correspondence.

Sigma Chi Fraternity v. George Mason University, ED Vir. No. 91-785-A. (1991).

Simon, W. (1987). Testing Freedom and Restraint. *Society, 24*(5), 27–30.

Singer, J. L., & Singer, D. (1981). *Television, Imagination and Aggression: A Study of Preschoolers*. Hillsdale, NJ: Erlbaum.

Singer, J., Singer, D., & Rapaczynski, W. (1984). Family Patterns and Television Viewing as Predictors of Children's Beliefs and Aggression. *Journal of Communications, 34*, 73–89.

Sipe, A. R. (1990). *A Secret World: Sexuality and the Search for Celibacy*. New York: Brunner-Mazel.

Sklar, R. (1976). *Movie-Made America: A Cultural History of the Movies*. New York: Random House.

Smith, M., Glass, G., & Miller, T. (1980). *The Benefits of Psychotherapy*. Baltimore, MD: Johns Hopkins University Press.

Smothers, R. (1988, November 15). Preacher's Journey: Long Trail of Abuse. *The New York Times*, pp. A1, A16.

Snitow, A., Stansell, C., & Thompson, S. (Eds.). (1983). *Powers of Desire: The Politics of Sexuality*. New York: Monthly Review Press.

Snitow, A. (1992). Personal communication.

Spring, J. (1992). *Images of American Life: A History of Ideological Management in Schools, Movies, Radio, and Television*. Albany: State University of New York Press.

Stanley, R. (1978). *The Celluloid Empire: A History of the American Movie Industry*. New York: Hastings House.

Steckler, D. (1989). Paper to the Fall Convention of the Virginia Psychological Association.

Steinfels, P. (1993, June 22). Pope Endorses Bishops' Attempts to Rid Clergy of Child Molesters. *The New York Times*, pp. A1, A14.

Stevenson, D. & Baker, D. (1987). The Family-School Relation and the Child's School Performance. *Child Development, 58*(5), 1348–1357.

Stevenson, V. (1990, December 12). Good News Communications Reveals Early Local Rating Board Targets. Los Angeles, New York: Motion Picture Association of America.

Strossen, N. (1990). Regulating Racist Speech on Campus: A Modest Proposal? *Duke Law Journal, 484*, 557.

Strossen, N. (1993). A Feminist Critique of "The" Feminist Critique of Pornography. *Virginia Law Review, 79*, pp. 1099–1190.

'Suicide' Bill Deserves to Lose. (1993, May 3). *Chicago Sun-Times*.

Sullivan, R. (1993, April 25). An Army of the Faithful. *The New York Times Magazine*, pp. 32–34, 40–44.

Surgeon General's Workshop on Pornography and Public Health, 1986. Report prepared by Edward Mulvey, Ph.D., Western Psychiatric Institute and Clinic, University of Pittsburgh, and Jeffrey Haugaard, M.A., Department of Psychology, University of Virginia. Arlington, VA: U.S. Department of Health and Human Services.

Taylor, J. K. (in press). Does Sexual Speech Harm Women? The Split Within Feminism. *Stanford Law and Policy Review, 5*(2).

Teller (1992, January 17). Movies Don't Cause Crime. *The New York Times*.

Thornburg, H. (1981). Adolescent Sources of Information on Sex. *The Journal of School Health, 51*, 274–277.

Tiefer, L. (1993, May 8). Paper to *Sex Panic: Women, Censorship and Pornography*. Symposium conducted by The National Coalition against Censorship, New York.

Trescott, J. (1993, June 22). Justice Defends 'Decency' Clause. *The Washington Post*, p. E7.

Twitchell, J. (1985). *Dreadful Pleasures. An Anatomy of Modern Horror*. Ch. 2, The Psychological Attraction of Horror. New York: Oxford University Press.

United Press International (1989, January 27). Bundy's Lawyer Decries Confessions.

U.S. Commission on Civil Rights (1974). *Women in Poverty*. Washington, DC: U.S. Government Printing Office.

U.S. Commission on Civil Rights (1979). *Women Still in Poverty*. Washington, DC: U.S. Government Printing Office.

U.S. Commission on Civil Rights (1981). *Child Care and Equal Opportunity for Women*. Washington. DC: U.S. Government Printing Office.

U.S. Commission on Obscenity and Pornography (1970). Technical Report. Washington, DC: U.S. Government Printing Office.

Valenti, J. (1987). *The Voluntary Movie Rating System: How It Began, Its Purpose, the Public Reaction*. New York/Los Angeles: The Motion Picture Association of America.

Valenti, J. (1993, July 1). Statement before the Subcommittee on Telecommunications, House Commerce Committee. Edward Markey, chair.

Vance, C. (Ed.). (1984). *Pleasure and Danger: Exploring Female Sexuality*. Boston: Routledge & Kegan Paul.

Varchaver, N. (1992, September). Protecting Women from Themselves? *The American Lawyer*.

Varian, N. (1989, July). Terry's Rights—and Yours. *Penthouse*, pp. 92–93.

Verna, P. (1991, March 15). Record Censorship Bills Back, Tougher Than Ever, RIAA says. *The Hollywood Reporter*, pp. 4, 89.

Vidal, G. (1993). *United States: Essays 1952–1992*. New York: Random House.

Walters, P., & Rubinson, R. (1983). Educational Expansion and Economic Output in the United States, 1890–1969: A Production Function Analysis. *American Sociological Review, 48*, 480–493.

Watters v. TSR, Inc., 904 F.2d 378 (6th Cir. 1990).

Weaver, J. (1987). Doctoral dissertation. University of Indiana, Bloomington, Indiana.

Webster, P. (1985, March 22). Paper to the Women in the Law Annual Conference, New York.

Weinrich, J. (1988). Interview, Society for the Scientific Study of Sex.

Wells, K. (1989, January 27). Did Pornography Influence Bundy? *St. Petersberg Times*, Floridian Section, p. 1D.

West Virginia State Board of Education v. Barnette, 319 U.S. 624, 642 (1943). Opinion by Justice Jackson.

Whicher, J. (1993). Constitutional and Policy Implications of 'Pornography Victim' Compensation Schemes. *Federal Bar News & Journal, 40(6)*, 360–367.

White, L. (1979). Erotica and Aggression: The Influence of Sexual Arousal, Positive Affect and Negative Affect on Aggressive Behavior. *Journal of Personality and Social Psychology, 37*, 591–601.

Wilcox, B. (1993, May 21). Statement before the Subcommittee on the Constitution, Committee of the Judiciary.

Wilkerson, I. (1990). Articles from September 24 to October 6. *The New York Times*.

Williams, B. (Ed.). (1973). *Science and Technology in Economic Growth*. New York: Wiley.

Williams, M. (1989, February 7). Bundy's Final Confession Fuels Porno Debate. *Chicago Tribune*, Tempo p. 1C.

Willis, E. (1981). Feminism, Moralism, and Pornography. In *Beginning to See the Light* (pp. 219–228). New York: Knopf.

Wilson, B., Linz, D., & Randall, B. (1990). Applying Social Science Research to Film Ratings: A Shift from Offensiveness to Harmful Effects. *Journal of Broadcasting & Electronic Media, 34(4)*, 443–468.

Winer, L. (1987, November 10). Limelight. *Newsday*, Part II, p. 6.

Witt, H. (1989, March 27). Priests' Sex Abuse Shocks Province. *Chicago Tribune*, section 1, p. 4.

WuDunn, S. (1990, December 29). China Ousts Two Aids and Raises Drug Penalties. *The New York Times,* p. A3.

Wurtzel, A., & Lometti, G. (1984). Researching Television Violence. *Society, 21*(6), 22–30.

Yaffee, M. (1982). Therapeutic uses of sexually explicit material. In M. Yaffee and E. Nelson (Eds.), *The Influence of Pornography on Behaviour.* (pp. 119–150). London: Academic Press.

Yang, N., & Linz, D. (1990). Movie Ratings and the Content of Adult Videos: The Sex–Violence Ratio. *Journal of Communication, 40*(2), 28–42.

Yardley, J. (1990, October 22). Art and the Oeuvre of 2 Live Crew. *The Washington Post*, p. B2.

Yardley, J. (1993, August 23–29). Code War on Expression. *The Washington Post National Weekly.*

Yolanda (1993, July). Personal communication.

Young, C. (1992, October). Victimhood Is Powerful. *Reason*, pp. 18–23.

Zillmann, D. (1979). *Hostility and Aggression.* Hillsdale, NJ: Erlbaum.

Zillmann, D. (1984). *Connections between Sex and Aggression.* Hillsdale, NJ: Erlbaum.

Zillmann, D., & Bryant, J. (1982). Pornography, Sexual Callousness, and the Trivialization of Rape. *Journal of Communication, 32*, 10–21.

Zillmann, D., & Bryant, J. (1984). Effects of Massive Exposure to Pornography. In N. Malamuth & E. Donnerstein (Eds.), *Pornography and Sexual Aggression* (pp.). New York: Academic Press.

Zillmann, D., & Bryant, J. (Eds.). (1989). *Pornography: Research Advances and Policy Considerations.* Hillsdale, NJ: Erlbaum.

Zillmann, D., & Sapolsky, B. (1977). What Mediates the Effect of Mild Erotica on Annoyance and Hostile Behavior in Males? *Journal of Personality and Social Psychology, 35*, pp. 587–596.

INDEX